MOTIVATION OF EXERCISE AND PHYSICAL ACTIVITY

MOTIVATION OF EXERCISE AND PHYSICAL ACTIVITY

LIAM A. CHIANG

EDITOR

Nova Science Publishers, Inc.

New York

NOTICE TO THE READER
The Publisher has taken reasonable care in the preparation of this book, but makes no expressed or implied warranty of any kind and assumes no responsibility for any errors or omissions. No liability is assumed for incidental or consequential damages in connection with or arising out of information contained in this book. The Publisher shall not be liable for any special, consequential, or exemplary damages resulting, in whole or in part, from the readers' use of, or reliance upon, this material.

Independent verification should be sought for any data, advice or recommendations contained in this book. In addition, no responsibility is assumed by the publisher for any injury and/or damage to persons or property arising from any methods, products, instructions, ideas or otherwise contained in this publication.

This publication is designed to provide accurate and authoritative information with regard to the subject matter covered herein. It is sold with the clear understanding that the Publisher is not engaged in rendering legal or any other professional services. If legal or any other expert assistance is required, the services of a competent person should be sought. FROM A DECLARATION OF PARTICIPANTS JOINTLY ADOPTED BY A COMMITTEE OF THE AMERICAN BAR ASSOCIATION AND A COMMITTEE OF PUBLISHERS.

LIBRARY OF CONGRESS CATALOGING-IN-PUBLICATION DATA

Motivation of exercise and physical activity / editor, Liam A. Chiang.
   p. ; cm.
 Includes bibliographical references and index.
   ISBN-13: 978-1-60021-596-4 (hardcover)
   ISBN-10: 1-60021-596-3 (hardcover)
   1. Exercise--Psychological aspects. 2. Motivation (Psychology) I. Chiang, Liam A.
   [DNLM: 1. Exercise--psychology. 2. Motivation. 3. Motor Activity--physiology. 4. Physical
Education and Training. QT 255 M918 2007]
GV706.4.M683 2007
796'.01--dc22   2007001365

Published by Nova Science Publishers, Inc. ✦ New York

CONTENTS

PREFACE

In psychology, motivation refers to the initiation, direction, intensity and persistence of behavior (Geen, 1995). Motivation is a temporal and dynamic state that should not be confused with personality or emotion. Motivation is having the desire and willingness to do something. A motivated person can be reaching for a long-term goal such as becoming a professional writer or a more short-term goal like learning how to spell a particular word. Personality invariably refers to more or less permanent characteristics of an individual's state of being (e.g., shy, extrovert, conscientious). As opposed to motivation, emotion refers to temporal states that do not immediately link to behavior (e.g., anger, grief, happiness). This new book focuses on motivation as related to exercise and physical activity.

Chapter 1 - Great athletes are a blend of talent and motivation. Talent is probably the most self-evident, easiest to see and measure. Motivation is harder to measure, but most coaches believe they can sense it. In my view, motivation requires nurturing and develops through three stages: detection, selection, and perfection. Motivation is first shown through various methods of detection. Sometimes motivation is self-discovered, but more often motivation is an outgrowth of enjoyment of the activity based on interactions with the coach and culture of the sport. Selection is a stage of further growth of motivation through the natural interactions of the athlete and sport and the selection of certain paths while avoiding others. Athletic perfection transcends talent and ambition alone, blending ability and desire in a self-reinforcing and artistic way that is both the lure and the satisfaction of high performance.

Chapter 2 - A study was conducted involving 882 Greek students who completed questionnaires on 3 occasions: 3-5 weeks into the academic year, 3-6 weeks before the end of the year and 7 months later. Perceived athletic competence both in the beginning of the academic year predicted sport and exercise participation 7 and 14 months later. Perceived athletic competence both at the beginning and end of the year predicted sport and exercise participation 7 and 14 months later, while ego orientation did not predict sport and exercise involvement at either time. Previous exercise participation had positive effects on task orientation and perceived athletic competence 3-6 weeks before the end of the academic year and predicted all cognitive-affective constructs 7 months later. These results imply that the cultivaton of task orientation, intrinsic motivation in physical education and perceived athletic competence will help to promote sport and exercise participation in adulthood.

Chapter 3 - The purpose of this study was to examine Vallerand's (2001) contention that perceptions of psychological need satisfaction underpin the endorsement of different motives, which in turn, predicts behavioural intentions in the context of exercise. Participants (N = 176; 51.2% female) involved in a group-based intramural event completed a self-administered cross-sectional survey comprised of demographic questions, the Psychological Need Satisfaction in Exercise Scale (PNSE; Wilson et al., 2006), the Behavioural Regulation in Exercise Questionnaire (BREQ; Mullan et al., 1997), and a behavioural intention scale (Courneya & McAuley, 1993). Bivariate correlations indicated stronger relationships between fulfillment of the psychological needs for competence, autonomy, and relatedness with identified and intrinsic regulations (r's ranged from 0.47 to 0.67) compared to external and introjected regulations (r's ranged from -0.30 to 0.19). Multivariate analysis using structural equation modeling supported the tenability of a model explaining behavioural intentions (R^2 = 0.17) as a function of a person's relative autonomy motivational index (γ = 41) which in turn was predicted by perceived competence (γ = 0.25), autonomy (γ = 0.53), and relatedness (γ = -0.12) in exercise contexts (χ^2 = 399.47; df = 183; CFI = 0.92; IFI = 0.92; $RMSEA$ = 0.08 [90% CI = 0.07 to 0.10]). Overall, the results of the present investigation partially support Vallerand's argument regarding the sequences that shape motivational processes in exercise contexts. Furthermore, the results of the present investigation provide support for the importance of psychological need satisfaction for internalized motivation in an applied context which is in line with more general arguments set forth within the framework of self-determination theory (Deci & Ryan, 1985; 2002).

Chapter 4 - Mapping the motivational structure of adolescents' physical activity behavior is a key point to the development of long term positive attitudes towards sports activity. Unfortunately, after the adolescent period, the level of physical activity seriously declines. However, as longitudinal studies have pointed out, the continuous and regular engagement in sports activity in childhood may increase the likelihood of exercising later in adulthood. Therefore, the main goal of the present study is to detect the motivational structure of early adolescents in distinct school districts in Szeged, Hungary, using a self-administered questionnaire (N=548). The response rate was 91%. Respondents were 10 to 15 years of age (Mean=12.2 years, S.D.=1.2 years) with 54.7 percent of the sample male and 44.9 percent female. A 5-point scale was used to measure the adolescents' motivational structure which contained 18 items derived from the Sport Motivation Scale (SMS). The scale involved both extrinsic and intrinsic types of motivation. Using factor analysis, a four-factor solution has been detected for early adolescents' sport related motivational structure: a "competition and achievement" motivational factor; a "physical fitness, health and sporting attitude" motivational factor; an "external requirements" motivational factor; and a "hedonistic" motivational factor. Both extrinsic and intrinsic motivations are present in the motivational structure of early adolescents related to physical activity. Some of the adolescents are motivated by competitions and prizes, whereas others are motivated by keeping healthy or increasing the level of physical fitness. Some of them are motivated by meeting the requirements of school or parents. In additon, even in this age group, some students are motivated by self-determination, having fun and enjoying the good companion during joint sports activity. Certain differences by sociodemographics and characteristics of sports activity could also be detected.

Chapter 5 - The purpose of the present study was to examine the effect of a life skills program taught in the school setting through physical education classes. The participants were 97 students (59 boys, 38 girls), aged from 10 to 12 years (M = 11,16, SD = .64). Students were evaluated regarding their: (a) performance in sport skills; (b) knowledge about life skills; (c) self – assessment of their ability to use life skills; and (d) their sense of self – efficiency about their sport skills performance before and after implementation of the program. The results of the study support the effectiveness of a program that integrates physical education curriculum and life- skills training. Students who participate in such program can improve their sports skills, while at the same time the inclusion of life skills training into practice may serve as an effective model for learning life – skills.

Chapter 6 - Coaches and fans alike know that a key factor in athletic team success is player motivation to perform well in game situations. For instance, basketball players must decide which shots to take and make wise decisions when they do so. The present study applied operant choice theory to understanding one facet of this decision. Operant choice theory addresses the problem of how individuals decide to distribute limited time and effort among mutually exclusive potential courses of action. The core assumption is that they do so based on expected consequences (in generic terms, reinforcement and punishment) associated with these actions. In the present study, we predicted shot selection (two-point versus three-point field goals) by players on eleven teams in a major college conference using a mathematical model of operant choice. Specifically, each player's ratio of two-point to three-point shots attempted was predicted as a function of the ratio of two-point to three-point shots made. This analysis is interesting in two respects. First, many people assume that operant principles, which have often been derived from research on nonhumans, have little to say about complex human behavior. Second, few kinds of behavior are as complex as those involved in elite sport competition, where a host of factors that are not included in our mathematical model are thought to apply. Nevertheless, our results strongly suggest that the choices players make are motivated by reinforcement. The choices players make are quite sensitive to the reinforcement for those choices and the model predicted most of the variance in shot selection among the players on each team. Whether shot selection contributes meaningfully to team success was considered in a follow-up analysis that used model fits to predict the winners of games in the season-ending league tournament. Overall, these results illustrate the broad generality of operant principles to everyday situations and suggests that these principles are quite robust in motivating behavior even in situations that are far more complex and dynamic than those studied in the laboratory.

Chapter 7 - This study examined whether similarities or differences between coaching and parenting behaviours are associated with cohesion in sport. The participants were Finnish ice hockey players of 14 and 16 years of age (N=1018) and their parents (N=979). The players rated their coaches using the Leadership Scale of Sport (LSS, Chelladurai & Saleh, 1980) and estimated team cohesion using a four-item scale that was prepared for the present study. Parents rated their own parenting behaviour using the Block's Child Rearing Practices Report (CRPR, Pulkkinen, 1996). Results revealed the importance of matching coaching and parenting that were associated with cohesion. In particular, the compensating combination of Non-Demanding styles at home and high support by the positive coach was associated with high cohesion. These results contribute to our understanding of the important relationship between, coach, parents and player, influencing cohesion and thus motivation at sport. This study is of relevance to coaches, teachers, and parents of young athletes.

Chapter 8 - Physical education is a critical site for addressing the twin epidemic of obesity and physical inactivity. It has been suggested that combining pedometer use with goal setting may be an effective way to foster exercise motivation and promote physical activity.

To date, research on this topic has focused on high school students and adults. The current study used a program evaluation framework and mixed methods to explore the feasibility of an upper elementary physical education pedometer program. Participants were 217 3rd (54), 4th (67), 5th (51), and 6th (45) grade boys and girls. Qualitative and quantitative findings support the notion that goal-based pedometer programs can be effectively implemented in the upper elementary grades. The effectiveness of the program did not appear to be mediated by gender or grade level. It is recommended that programs of this type be introduced to pre-adolescent populations through school-based physical education to address growing rates of physical inactivity and obesity. Future studies should explore the impact of such programs on the actual activity levels, relevant psychological constructs, and future health status of participants.

Chapter 9 - The purpose of this study was to investigate the univariate and multivariate relationships among an individual's dispositional goal orientation (task/ego), classroom motivational climate (mastery/performance), and pleasant or unpleasant psychobiosocial (PBS) states (i.e., emotion, cognition, motivation, bodily reactions, movement, performance, and communication) as conceptualized within the Individual Zones of Optimal Functioning model. The participants were 1632 Italian physical education pupils (809 girls and 823 boys, aged 11-14 years) drawn from public junior high schools. The assessment included a goal orientation questionnaire, a motivational climate inventory, and pleasant and unpleasant PBS descriptors. Hierarchical multiple regression analysis showed that an individual's task orientation was directly related to pleasant PSB states and indirectly related to unpleasant PBS states. Canonical correlation analysis indicated that task-oriented students who perceived a mastery-involving climate tended to experience high levels of pleasant states and low levels of unpleasant states. Findings suggest that physical education teachers should create a motivational mastery climate, thereby promoting task involvement and a pleasant emotional experience.

In: Motivation of Exercise and Physical Activity
Editor: Liam A. Chiang, pp. 1-6

ISBN: 978-1-60021-596-4
© 2007 Nova Science Publishers, Inc.

Expert Commentary

THE CONCEPTUALIZATION OF THE STAGES OF PHYSICAL ACTIVITY CHANGE AMONG PEOPLE WITH PHYSICAL DISABILITIES

Maria Kosma[*]

Louisiana State University, Department of Kinesiology, 112 H.P. Long Fieldhouse, Room 55, Baton Rouge, LA 70803, USA

Although the benefits of regular physical activity participation are well documented, 56% of adults with physical disabilities (e.g., spinal cord injury, multiple sclerosis, and cerebral palsy) do not participate in any leisure-time physical activity compared with 36% of adults without disabilities. Additionally, individuals with disabilities tend to report lower health-related quality of life (HRQOL; physical and mental health) levels than people without disabilities (United States Department of Health and Human Services, [USDHHS], 2000). The importance of determining theory-based factors that motivate individuals with disabilities to be physically active and thus increase their HRQOL has been recognized (Grodesky, Kosma, & Solmon, 2006; Kosma, Cardinal, & McCubbin, 2005; Kosma, Cardinal, & Rintala, 2002; Kosma, Ellis Gardner, Cardinal, Bauer, & McCubbin, 2006, in press; USDHHS, 2000). Using an integrative framework whereby constructs of the Theory of Planned Behavior (TPB) are integrated with the stages of change (SOC) of the Transtheoretical Model (TTM) may facilitate progress in this area (Grodesky, Kosma, & Solmon, 2006; Kosma et al., 2006, in press).

Based on the TPB (Ajzen, 1991; see Figure 1), the major determinant of physical activity is intention (motivation to be active). Intention is influenced by attitude (perceived consequences of physical activity), subjective norm (perceived social pressure to be active from significant others), and perceived behavioral control (PBC; perceived confidence and control of physical activity). Attitude, subjective norm, and PBC are hypothesized to affect physical activity indirectly through intention. Perceived behavioral control is also stipulated to directly affect behavior.

[*] Email: mkosma@lsu.edu; Phone: (225) 578-8016; Fax: (225) 578-3680

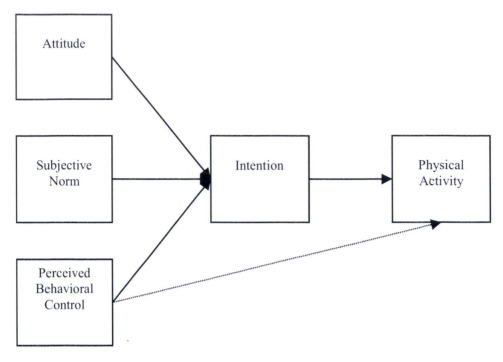

Figure 1. The Conceptual Model of TPB (Ajzen, 1991).

Overall, the predictive strength of the TPB for physical activity among mainly individuals without disabilities has been supported. Specifically, in a recent meta-analysis of the TPB and physical activity (Downs & Hausenblas, 2005), the most important predictor of physical activity was intention and the most important predictors of intention were attitude and PBC among people without disabilities. Similar findings were reported in a recent study that applied the TPB for physical activity among adults with physical disabilities (Ellis Gardner, Kosma, Cardinal, Bauer, & McCubbin, 2006).

The TTM is an integrative framework whereby the SOC, processes of change, self-efficacy, and decisional balance influence physical activity (Prochaska & Velicer, 1997). The processes of change reflect cognitive strategies (e.g., perceived importance of physical activity) and behavioral strategies (e.g., social support) people use to be active. Decisional balance refers to the balance between the perceived pros (benefits) and cons (costs) of physical activity. If the perceived pros outweigh the perceived cons then the likelihood of physical activity participation increases. Self-efficacy represents the perceived ability to overcome physical activity barriers and maintain an active lifestyle.

A major dimension of the TTM is the SOC (Prochaska & Velicer, 1997), which reflect both intention and behavior (Kosma et al., in press; Marcus, Eaton, Rossi, & Harlow, 1994; Nigg, 2005; Rosen, 2000). Examining both behavior and intention may increase the predictive strength of the SOC for physical activity behavior (Kosma et al., in press; Rosen, 2000). Individuals can be classified within five SOC: a) precontemplation (inactivity and lack of physical activity intention), b) contemplation (inactivity and intention to be active within six months), c) preparation (irregularly active and intention to be active within one month), d) action (regularly active for less than 6 months), and e) maintenance (regularly active for more than 6 months). Physical activity motivational programs tailored toward an individual's SOC (stage-matched programs) are reported to be more effective on positive physical activity behavior change than stage-mismatched programs for college personnel (Blissmer & McAuley, 2002).

Although the conceptual definition of the SOC reflects both intention and behavior, the current SOC measures do not incorporate *both* intention and behavior within each stage. Specifically, in a recommended SOC algorithm (Reed, Velicer, Prochaska, Rossi, & Marcus, 1997) the terminology of the early SOC (e.g., planning to be active) may not directly reflect intention. Additionally, it has been critiqued that the early SOC do not measure physical activity behavior and the later SOC (action and maintenance) do not directly reflect intention (Godin, Lambert, Owen, Nolin, & Prud'homme, 2004). Therefore, the construct validity of a modified SOC scale (see Appendix 1) needs to be tested among such an understudied population as people with physical disabilities. In this scale, the long definition of physical activity is captured using physical activity types that relate to the population of interest (adults with physical disabilities; Reed et al., 1997). Both physical activity intention and physical activity behavior are assessed within each stage (Godin et al., 2004). The 5-choice response format is used to classify individuals within each stage (Reed et al., 1997).

The construct validity of the proposed SOC scale (see Appendix 1) can be tested by examining the relations among the SOC, physical activity, the constructs of the TTM (i.e., processes of change, self-efficacy, and decisional balance), and HRQOL among adults with physical disabilities. To secure construct validity, the processes of change along with self-efficacy, perceived pros, physical activity, and HRQOL need to increase across the SOC. Perceived cons are expected to decrease across the SOC (Kosma et al., 2006).

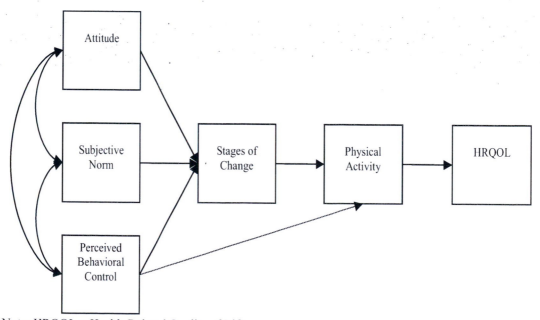

Note: HRQOL = Health-Related Quality of Life.

Figure 2. An Integrative Framework of Physical Activity for Health and Wellness.

The construct validity of the reported SOC scale (see Appendix 1) can also be tested by examining the mediating role of past SOC in future physical activity and HRQOL using advanced statistical techniques (e.g., path analysis). Specifically, the SOC are stipulated to mediate the relation between the TPB constructs (attitude, subjective norm, and PBC) and physical activity among adults with physical disabilities (Kosma et al., in press). In the 6-month prospective study of Kosma et al. (in press), a path analysis was used to compare the TPB model with an integrative framework (TPB/SOC), whereby the SOC scale of Reed et al. (1997) replaced intention in the TPB. Past SOC was a stronger predictor of future physical activity than past intention. Additionally, the most important predictor of the SOC was attitude followed by PBC. Subjective norm did not have a significant effect on the SOC. Using the proposed SOC scale (see Appendix 1), that reflects both intention and behavior within each stage, the predictive strength of the SOC for future physical activity and HRQOL may increase (see Figure 2).

APPENDIX 1
STAGES OF PHYSICAL ACTIVITY CHANGE SCALE FOR ADULTS WITH PHYSICAL DISABILITIES

Regular physical activity should be performed on most, if not all days of the week, for an accumulation of 30 minutes, and of moderate or higher intensity. Such activities include walking (with or without crutches, canes, braces, or prostheses), jogging, off-road pushing, ball games (e.g., doubles and/or singles tennis, softball, basketball, golf without a cart), swimming, cycling, arm cranking, dancing, and other similar activities. Activities that are primarily sedentary, such as bowling, playing golf with a cart, and passive stretching, are NOT considered regular physical activity.

Instructions

According to the above definition of "regular physical activity", please check one of the following statements that best pertains to your case:

☐ I have been physically active for less than once per week and I do not intend to be regularly physically active in the next 6 months.

☐ I have been physically active about once a week and I do not intend to be regularly physically active in the next month.

☐ I have been physically active about once a week and I intend to be regularly physically active in the next month.

☐ I have been physically active three times per week or more and I intend to be regularly physically active in the next month.

Stage Classification

Stage 1: Inactive
Stage 2: Preparator unconcerned
Stage 3: Preparator concerned
Stage 4: Active

REFERENCES

Ajzen, I. (1991). The Theory of Planned Behavior. *Organizational Behavior and Human Decision Processes, 50*, 179-211.

Blissmer, B., & McAuley, E. (2002). Testing the requirements of stages of physical activity among adults: The comparative effectiveness of stage-matched, mismatched, standard care, and control interventions. *Annals of Behavioral Medicine, 24*, 181-189.

Downs, D.S., & Hausenblas, H.A. (2005). The Theories of Reasoned Action and Planned Behavior applied to exercise: A meta-analytic update. *Journal of Physical Activity and Health, 2*, 76-97.

Ellis Gardner, R., Kosma, M., Cardinal, B.J., Bauer, J.J., & McCubbin, J.A. (2006). *A comparison of two models assessing physical activity participation among adults with physical disabilities: Testing the Theory of Planned Behavior.* Manuscript submitted for publication.

Godin, G., Lambert, L.D., Owen, N., Nolin, B., & Prud'homme, D. (2004). Stages of motivational readiness for physical activity: A comparison of different algorithms of classification. *British Journal of Health Psychology, 9*, 253-267.

Grodesky, J.M., Kosma, M., & Solmon, M.A. (2006). Understanding older adults' physical activity behavior: A multi-theoretical approach. *Quest, 58,* 310-329.

Kosma, M., Cardinal, B.J., & McCubbin, J.A. (2005). A pilot study of a web-based physical activity motivational program for adults with physical disabilities. *Disability and Rehabilitation: An International Multidisciplinary Journal, 27*, 1435-1442.

Kosma, M., Cardinal, B.J., & Rintala, P. (2002). Motivating individuals with disabilities to be physically active. *Quest, 54*, 116-132.

Kosma, M., Ellis Gardner, R., Cardinal, B.J., Bauer, J.J., & McCubbin, J.A. (2006). Psychosocial determinants of stages of change and physical activity among adults with physical disabilities. *Adapted Physical Activity Quarterly, 23*, 49-64.

Kosma, M., Ellis Gardner, R., Cardinal, B.J., Bauer, J.J., & McCubbin, J.A. (in press). The mediating role of intention and stages of change in physical activity among adults with physical disabilities: An integrative framework. *Journal of Sport and Exercise Psychology.*

Marcus, B.H., Eaton, C.A., Rossi, J.S., & Harlow, L.L. (1994). Self-efficacy, decision-making, and stages of change: An integrative model of physical exercise. *Journal of Applied Social Psychology, 24*, 489-508.

Nigg, C.R. (2005). There is more to stages of exercise than just exercise. *Exercise and Sport Sciences Reviews, 33*, 32-35.

Prochaska, J.O., & Velicer, W.F. (1997). The Transtheoretical Model of health behavior change. *American Journal of Health Promotion, 12*, 38-48.

Reed, G.R., Velicer, W.F., Prochaska, J.O., Rossi, J.S., & Marcus, B.H. (1997). What makes a good staging algorithm: Examples from regular exercise. *American Journal of Health Promotion, 12*, 57-66.

Rosen, C.S. (2000). Integrating stage and continuum models to explain processing of exercise messages and exercise initiation among sedentary college students. *Health Psychology, 19*, 172-180.

U.S. Department of Health and Human Services. (2000). Physical activity and fitness. In Healthy People 2010 (2nd ed.). *With understanding and improving health and objectives for improving health* (Vols. 1-2), Washington, DC: U.S. Government Printing Office.

In: Motivation of Exercise and Physical Activity
Editor: Liam A. Chiang, pp. 7-12

ISBN: 978-1-60021-596-4
© 2007 Nova Science Publishers, Inc.

Chapter 1

DETECTION, SELECTION, PERFECTION – AN OPINION PAPER

Wm. A. Sands

Recovery Center, Biomechanics and Engineering, U.S. Olympic Committee,
Performance Services, 1 Olympic Plaza, Colorado Springs, CO 80909, USA

ABSTRACT

Great athletes are a blend of talent and motivation. Talent is probably the most self-evident, easiest to see and measure. Motivation is harder to measure, but most coaches believe they can sense it. In my view, motivation requires nurturing and develops through three stages: detection, selection, and perfection. Motivation is first shown through various methods of detection. Sometimes motivation is self-discovered, but more often motivation is an outgrowth of enjoyment of the activity based on interactions with the coach and culture of the sport. Selection is a stage of further growth of motivation through the natural interactions of the athlete and sport and the selection of certain paths while avoiding others. Athletic perfection transcends talent and ambition alone, blending ability and desire in a self-reinforcing and artistic way that is both the lure and the satisfaction of high performance.

When you ask coaches, "What do you want most in an athlete?" Coaches will often respond, "I want an athlete who is *motivated*." When you ask an athlete what he or she wants most in a coach, he/she often responds, "I want a coach who can *motivate* me." It should be clear that motivation is highly prized and a valuable part of sport. However, identifying who is responsible or who leads is often not clear. Moreover, determining exactly what motivation is can be both difficult and confusing (Miner, 1995), yet nearly every coach believes that he/she can recognize it. Does motivation come from the leaders? Does motivation come from the athletes? Does motivation begin with leadership and then shift to the athlete, or vice versa? Can motivation be taught or do you have to find it and then nurture it? Something short of teaching but more than genetically determined.

Sport makes special efforts to identify those people who not only have the physical tools, but also the motivation or need for achievement that will take them to the highest levels of performance. Sport is an astonishing laboratory for the study of motivation. As the author of the oldest and most mature talent identification program in the U.S. (Sands, 1993), the idea of motivation, achievement orientation, and potential for high performance were integral parts of the initial planning of the Talent Opportunity Program for USA Gymnastics (then the United States Gymnastics Federation). The Talent Opportunity Program (TOPs) now tests between two and three thousand aspiring young female gymnasts each year (Warren, 1995). A battery of tests, administered at state, regional, and national levels is used to differentiate and rank athletes in an attempt to identify those young gymnasts between the ages of 9 and 11 or 12 years who have the physical abilities, skills, talents, and motivation necessary to achieve in gymnastics at the highest levels.

The idea of talent identification is not new to sport, nor is the concern for identifying those youngsters with the appropriate motivation to excel. Events and programs from the TOPs program in gymnastics to the NFL Combines use various physical tests along with actual sport performance to detect, select, and later perfect the athlete (Russell, 1987). In professional sports, there is an entire industry within an industry that scouts, analyzes and attempts to identify the constellation of factors that lead to high performance. While this may seem somewhat mercenary with children, the idea of helping youngsters identify those sports in which they might excel is simply more efficient and may help direct a youngster to a sport that he or she would not have thought of prior to the determination of aptitude (Bompa, 1985).

Indeed, it is rare for a youngster to wake up one morning with a burning desire to be a rower, luger, modern pentathlete, or other relatively obscure sport. Many youngsters grow up with an extreme desire or motivation to be a great football, basketball, baseball, or hockey player – yet only an almost vanishingly small percentage will ever achieve such goals. When questioned about the sport machine of the former East Germany, the athletes who were products of that machine often point to the fact that they came from a relatively poor family, yet by virtue of early selection they could excel in what might be considered upper class sports in the West, such as figure skating (Gilbert, 1980). Clearly, some athletes in the West with the requisite motivation and physical tools are left to spectate because they simply cannot afford the cost of training or otherwise become an enormous economic burden on their family (Bungum, Wald, & Martin, 2000). There are numerous paradoxes in sport motivation that demand both study and explanation (Hatfield & Brody, 1994; Henschen, Sands, Gordin, & Martinez, 1990; Raglin, Morgan, & Luchsinger, 1990; Roberts & McKelvain, 1987; Rodgers & Brawley, 1991; Rotella, 1983). What might we learn from sport that could assist others in understanding how motivation might be observed, measured, predicted, and nurtured?

Let's begin with the idea of coaching and motivation. First and foremost, coaching is teaching (Sands, 1984). Coaches are well aware of the differences between motivated and unmotivated athletes. A common coaching lament is, "this athlete has all the physical tools but no motivation." Such phrases as "killer instinct," "sheer aggressiveness," and "reckless abandon" are commonly used to describe the extremes of motivation. The tacit understanding that these extremes are desirable permeates much of sport. How do coaches teach this? Or, do they teach it at all?

DETECTION

In over 40 years of involvement in sport with more than 30 years at the highest Olympic levels, I believe that motivation is not taught in the conventional sense. You don't start without motivation and then after some teaching suddenly "have it." Motivation is not like a physical skill. In my opinion, coaches seek those athletes who already demonstrate high levels of motivation – they detect them. Athletes who are highly motivated are not hard to find, they populate almost every sport venue. Finding the highly motivated is not a problem. Finding the highest motivation is. Combining the highest motivation with the highest levels of physical tools is every coach's dream; one cannot be successful without the other. The detection process, at least in the U.S. is largely built upon long-term attrition in the caldron of competition. However, not every highly motivated and highly skilled athlete makes it. Clearly, the recipe for high level success is not as simple as asking people if they're highly motivated.

SELECTION

If athletes are highly skilled and highly motivated, and perhaps among those who could make it to the highest levels – what might stop them? Certainly injury is a deterrent along with poverty, genetic background, and place of birth. You don't see many great alpine skiers from Costa Rica. You don't see many great basketball players from the Kalahari. This is not because Costa Ricans can't ski or because residents of the Kalahari can't learn to play basketball, there are just very limited opportunities without making extremely expensive and diligent efforts. In sport, motivation must be married to opportunity. It may be politically incorrect to discuss such issues, but the issues doggedly remain (Entine, 2000). There are numerous examples of the role of genetic background in modern high performance sport (Bouchard, 1986; Bouchard, Malina, & Perusse, 1997; Malina, 1986; Malina, 1988; Montgomery et al., 1998; Roberts, 1986; Unal & Ozer Unal, 2004). Yet, even genetics can be stymied despite either gifted or deprived genetic backgrounds. Why? I believe the primary difference is "selection." All of the things listed above and many more serve as selection "pressures" that push or drive the contingencies and incumbencies of any "sport-historical" sequence (Gould, 1989; Sands & McNeal, 2000; Shermer, 1996). Rarely but often memorably, the competitive scales are tipped in unanticipated directions. The genetic, talent, and perhaps unlucky underdog beats the more impressive and favored champion. Physical tools, acquired by genetics, maturity, and training are necessary but insufficient to fulfill the goals of high achievement. Motivation, by itself, is necessary but insufficient to fulfill the same goals. Hollywood has probably made billions dramatizing such epics from the 1980 Miracle Hockey Team to the Rocky series.

Selection pressures begin in the family with children often favoring the sports that their parents played, or perhaps more important in an age of rampant obesity, simply adopting a parental example of active living. Others have aptly described the stages through which talent is developed while touching on motivation (Bajin, 1986; Bloom, 1985; Dick, 1992; Drabik, 1996; Hohmann & Seidel, 2003; Holden. C., 2004). While initial exposures to sports may be somewhat random, the process that follows seldom is.

In the earliest stage of development the young athlete is usually exposed to a coach or teacher who lacks technical development knowledge but simply loves the sport *and* children. The child learns to love the sport largely through an outgrowth of his/her fondness for the teacher/coach and/or the culture that teacher/coach creates around the sport. Motivation is nurtured unconsciously due to the close proximity of the sport to the acts of play. A second stage usually occurs when the athlete shifts to a coach with much greater technical knowledge who hones the athlete's abilities and continues to nurture the athlete's motivation. However, the athlete's motivation is now both different in kind and in quantity due to a need for achievement (Miner, 1995). The athlete may seek achievement via pleasing him/herself, the coach, parents, friends, and simply to be very good at something. In this stage the coach is more of a comrade, certainly heavily involved with the athlete as he/she travels the path of development together, but not a friend. The athlete learns about motivation by watching other athletes and by old-fashioned Skinnerian-type conditioning where important and desirable behaviors are rewarded with some type of praise, attention, or award and those behaviors that are undesirable are punished, at times harshly (Hoberman, 1992; Hodge & Tod, 1993). The reward and punishment type of approach to motivation is not unique to sport, having also been described in realms such as higher education (Sacks, 1996; Sykes, 1988). The selection period lasts a relatively long time and embodies much of the education of the young athlete in all aspects of the sport, especially motivation. Eventually, the athlete reaches a mature state when he/she is an independent functioning athlete who chooses to participate or not, excel or not, win or not. The coach's "teaching" is largely over and the athlete has dominant control of his or her performance.

PERFECTION

As the athlete progresses through the selection pressures and succumbs and rises to the various forces that drive him/her to find his/her place in sport, the third aspect of motivation development occurs. The final aspect of motivation is perfection. Although perfection may be logically impossible to achieve, certainly great athletes can achieve an "empirical best." Even this "near-perfection" is often fleeting and ephemeral but the personal sense of harmony it evokes is often what transforms athletes into artists and provides an almost spiritual experience for the athlete and vicarious wonderment for the spectator. Athletes at this stage are more artists than competitors, competing with their opponents rather than against. Coaches become more of a resource and critic than technician. It is a very rare coach who can deal with all stages of an athlete's development. Usually, coaches specialize in one area, consciously or unconsciously. Some coaches are great with beginners but are intimidated by the higher levels of technical knowledge required to really excel. Technicians are often so concerned about technique that they don't allow the athlete to mature to independence. The final perfection stage of the athlete is where his/her style becomes manifest, where the athlete's perceptions of his/her actions seem to bend time, and the best performances feel effortless rather than enormously taxing.

Motivation takes on a new character during the perfection stage. There is an almost addictive desire to achieve that special place where all aspects of performance come together in a symbiotic whole that puts the athlete at the very top of his or her game. Studying motivation at this level is much like studying meteor impacts – you have to wait for one to happen and then hope you're in the right place when it does. Motivation at this stage is almost entirely from within. A coach may be able to direct the object of motivation somewhat, but has little control over its initiation or final direction.

CONCLUSION

Motivation is a topic that involves a great deal of rhetoric, considerable analysis via description and some forms of research aptly labeled theories. Theories are not "junior laws" that someday grow up to be "real laws." Theories are explanations. Everything from Self-Efficacy Theory by Bandura to McClelland's Theory of Needs has attempted to characterize the dimensions of motivation. Sport provides a marvelous laboratory to study motivation, and in the end I think athletes may be the ideal subjects for both investigation and receipt of motivation theories and practices. Moreover, in the end, I believe that motivation is not really taught but captured in an early and relatively pure form to be later molded by the athlete, coach, environment, and circumstances.

REFERENCES

Bajin, B. (1986). Talent identification programs for Canadian female gymnasts. B. Petiot, J. H. Salmela, & T. B. Hoshizaki *World Identification Systems for Gymnastic Talent* (pp. 34-44). Montreal, Canada: Sport Psyche Publications.

Bloom, B. S. (1985). Developing talent in young people. B. S. Bloom (pp. 507-549). New York, NY: Ballantine Books.

Bompa, T. O. (1985). Talent identification. *Science Periodical on Research and Technology in Sport,* 1-11.

Bouchard, C. (1986). Genetics of aerobic power and capacity. R. M. Malina, & C. Bouchard *Sport and human genetics* (4 ed., pp. 59-88). Champaign, IL: Human Kinetics.

Bouchard, C., Malina, R. M., & Perusse, L. (1997). *Genetics of fitness and physical performance.* Champaign, IL: Human Kinetics.

Bungum, T. J., Wald, J., & Martin, S. (2000). Parental motivation for supporting their children's involvement in a private gymnastic program. *Medicine and Science in Sports and Exercise, 32*(5), S95.

Dick, F. (1992). Winners are made - not born. *New Studies in Athletics, 7*(3), 13-17.

Drabik, J. (1996). *Children & sports training.* Island Pond, VT: Stadion Publishing Co.

Entine, J. (2000). *Taboo.* New York, NY: PublicAffairs.

Gilbert, D. (1980). *The miracle machine.* New York, NY: Coward, McCann & Geoghegan, Inc.

Gould, S. J. (1989). George Canning's left buttock and the origin of species. *Natural History, 5,* 18-23.

Hatfield, B. D., & Brody, E. B. (1994). The psychology of athletic preparation and performance: The mental management of physical resources. T. R. Baechle *Essentials of strength training and conditioning* (pp. 163-187). Champaign, IL: Human Kinetics.

Henschen, K., Sands, W. A., Gordin, R., & Martinez, R. (1990). Psychological differences between Olympic gymnasts and the remainder of the senior national team. *Technique, 10*(3), 4-5, 23.

Hoberman, J. (1992). *Mortal engines*. New York, NY: Free Press.

Hodge, K. P., & Tod, D. A. (1993). Ethics of childhood sport. *Sports Medicine, 15*(5), 291-298.

Hohmann, A., & Seidel, I. (2003). Scientific aspects of talent development. *Sport Science Studies, 40*(1), 9-20.

Holden. C. (2004). Peering under the hood of Africa's runners. *Science, 305*(5684), 637-639.

Malina, R. M. (1986). Genetics of motor development and performance. R. M. Malina, & C. Bouchard *Sport and human genetics* (4 ed., pp. 23-58). Champaign, IL: Human Kinetics.

Malina, R. M. (1988). Racial/ethnic variation in the motor development and performance of American children. *Canadian Journal of Sport Science, 13*(2), 136-143.

Miner, M. J. (1995). Motivation in sport. K. P. Henschen, & W. F. Straub *Sport Psychology an Analysis of Athlete Behavior* (3rd ed., pp. 63-70). Longmeadow, MA: Mouvement Publications.

Montgomery, H. E., Marshall, R., Hemingway, H., Myerson, S., Clarkson, P., Dollery, C., Hayward, M., Hollimann, D. E., Jubb, M., World, M., Thomas, E. L., Brynes, A. E., Saeed, N., Barnard, M., Bell, J. D., Prasad, K., Rayson, M., Talmud, P. J., & Humphries, S. E. (1998). Human gene for physical performance. *Nature, 393*, 221.

Raglin, J. S., Morgan, W. P., & Luchsinger, A. E. (1990). Mood and self-motivation in successful and unsuccessful female rowers. *Medicine and Science in Sports and Exercise, 22*(6), 849-853.

Roberts, D. F. (1986). Genetic determinants of sports performance. R. M. Malina, & C. Bouchard *Sport and human genetics* (4 ed., pp. 105-121). Champaign, IL: Human Kinetics.

Roberts, G. C., & McKelvain, R. (1987). Motivational goals of elite young gymnasts. J. H. Salmela, B. Petiot, & T. B. Hoshizaki *Psychological nurturing and guidance of gymnastic talent* (pp. 186-193). Montreal, Canada: Sport Psyche Editions.

Rodgers, W. M., & Brawley, L. R. (1991). The role of outcome expectancies in participation motivation. *Journal of Sport & Exercise Psychology, 13*, 411-427.

Rotella, R. J. (1983). Motivational concerns of high level gymnasts. L. Unestahl *The mental aspects of gymnastics* (pp. 67-85). Orebro, Sweden: Veje Publishers.

Russell, K. (1987). Gymnastic talent from detection to perfection. B. Petiot, J. H. Salmela, & T. B. Hoshizaki *World identification systems for gymnastic talent* (pp. 4-13). Montreal, Canada: Sport Psyche Editions.

Sacks, P. (1996). *Generation X goes to college*. Chicago, IL: Open Court.

Sands, B. (1984). *Coaching women's gymnastics*. Champaign, IL: Human Kinetics.

Sands, W. A. (1993). *Talent opportunity program*. Indianapolis, IN: United States Gymnastics Federation.

Sands, W. A., & McNeal, J. R. (2000). Predicting athlete preparation and performance: A theoretical perspective. *Journal of Sport Behavior, 23(2)*, 1-22.

Shermer, M. (1996). Gould's dangerous idea. *Skeptic, 4*(1), 91-95.

Sykes, C. J. (1988). *Profscam*. New York, NY: St. Martin's Press.

Unal, M., & Ozer Unal, D. (2004). Gene doping in sports. *Sports Medicine, 34*(6), 357-362.

Warren, G. (1995). 1994 National TOPs Report. *Technique, 16(1)*, 38-39.

In: Motivation of Exercise and Physical Activity
Editor: Liam A. Chiang, pp. 13-33

ISBN: 978-1-60021-596-4
© 2007 Nova Science Publishers, Inc.

Chapter 2

RELATIONSHIPS OF SPORT AND EXERCISE INVOLVEMENT WITH GOAL ORIENTATIONS, PERCEIVED COMPETENCE AND INTRINSIC MOTIVATION IN PHYSICAL EDUCATION CLASSES

E. Bebetsos

Dept. of Phy. Education & Sport Science, Democritus University,
Komotini, Hellas

ABSTRACT

A study was conducted involving 882 Greek students who completed questionnaires on 3 occasions: 3-5 weeks into the academic year, 3-6 weeks before the end of the year and 7 months later. Perceived athletic competence both in the beginning of the academic year predicted sport and exercise participation 7 and 14 months later. Perceived athletic competence both at the beginning and end of the year predicted sport and exercise participation 7 and 14 months later, while ego orientation did not predict sport and exercise involvement at either time. Previous exercise participation had positive effects on task orientation and perceived athletic competence 3-6 weeks before the end of the academic year and predicted all cognitive-affective constructs 7 months later. These results imply that the cultivaton of task orientation, intrinsic motivation in physical education and perceived athletic competence will help to promote sport and exercise participation in adulthood.

INTRODUCTION

Regular exercise has many health benefits in adolescence and adulthood (Biddle, Sallis, & Cavill, 1998; Bouchard, Shephard, & Stephens, 1994). A number of intrapersonal, social and environmental variables have been identified as determinants of exercise in children and adolescents (Sallis & Owen, 1998). Several psychological variables have been shown to reduce the likelihood that adolescents will engage in exercise, including low self-efficacy (Reynolds et al., 1990; Trost et al, 1997), perceived barriers such as lack of time and lack of interest (Tappe, Duda, & Ehmwald, 1989), a dislike of physical education (Zakarian, Hovell, Hofstetter, Sallis, & Keating, 1994) and low enjoinment (Sallis, Prochaska, Taylor, Hill, & Geraci, 1999; Stucky-Ropp & DiLorenzo, 1993). Perceived athletic competence (Fox & Corbin, 1989), goal orientations (Duda, 2001) and intrinsic motivation (Vallerand & Rousseau, 2001) are considered to be important determinants of achievement behaviours such as persistence in sport. Nevertheless, little research has examined the prospective effects of perceived athletic competence and goal orientations in exercise in adolescence. The association of participation in physical activity with perceived athletic competence and goal orientations is mostly based on cross-sectional data that cannot imply causality (e.g. Fox, Goudas, Biddle, Duda, & Armstrong, 1994). The lack of available research suggesting causality is possibly a cause for the exclusion of goal orientations and perceived athletic competence from epidemiologists' lists of determinants of physical activity in youth (e.g. Sallis & Owen, 1998, p. 129). In addition, not enough studies have examined the causal relationship between out-of-school participation in sport and exercise and intrinsic motivation in physical education (Hagger, Chatzisarantis, Culverhouse, & Biddle, 2003). The present study examined the causal relationship of sport and exercise participation with goal orientations, perceived athletic competence and intrinsic motivation in physical education in a nationally representative sample of Greek adolescents.

All theories of motivation underline the positive role of perceived competence and self-esteem in human motivation (e.g. Bandura, 1986; Deci & Ryan, 1985, Harter, 1978; Weiner, 1985). High perceived competence facilitates positive expectations for success and achievement behaviours such as persistence, choice of challenging tasks and high effort. Research has shown that general self-esteem is unrelated to sport and exercise involvement (Sallis et al., 1992). On the other hand, physical self-esteem is considered an important correlate of engagement in sport and exercise contexts (Fox & Corbin, 1989; Weiss, Bredemeier, & Shewchuk, 1986). Nevertheless, research has yet to establish the causality between physical self-esteem and sport and exercise participation. One should expect that youngsters who participate in sport, to develop their athletic abilities and this should have positive effects on their perceptions of sport competence (Bandura, 1986). Hence, bi-directional effects should be expected between perceived athletic competence and participation in sport and exercise. In addition to perceptions of competence, achievement goals are also considered important correlates of achievement behaviours such as participation in sport (Duda, 1989). Nicholls (1984), Dweck (1986) and others (Ames, 1992; Elliot & Church, 1997; Maehr & Nicholls, 1980) developed a theory according to which achievement goals are conceptualized as the purpose (Maehr, 1989) or cognitive focus (Elliot & Church, 1997) of task engagement, and the type of goal adopted is presumed to create a framework of how people interpret, expedience and act in achievement settings. Most of this research focused on two types of goals: task orientation (also labelled mastery and learning goals), or the goal of developing one's competence and task mastery, and ego orientation (also called performance or ability goals), or the demonstration of one's competence relevant to others.

It is widely accepted that task orientation is positively linked with adaptive behaviours in physical activity settings (Duda & Hall, 2001; Roberts, 2001), but it is unclear whether there is unanimous agreement about the role of ego orientation. Hardy (1997) suggested that ego orientation facilitates achievement behaviours in elite sport in particular because ego orientation matches the competitive nature of sport. Duda (1997) does not agree with this view, who argued that this could only happen when ego orientation is accompanied by high perceived athletic competence. According to achievement goal theorists (Elliot & Dweck, 1988; Nicholls, 1984), high ego-oriented individuals are likely to expect success and positive feelings when they also have high perceptions of ability. On the other hand, when task orientation is high, individuals both high and low in perceived competence sustain positive expectations, expedience positive affect and employ adaptive strategies in achievement settings. Indeed, recent reviews (e.g. Duda & Hall, 2001) and meta-analyses (e.g. Ntoumanis & Biddle, 1999) including many studies have supported the positive impact of task orientation on several adaptive values, affects and coping strategies in sport. In sum, these sport-related cognitive-affective patterns are supposed to cultivate youth sport involvement. Duda and Hall (2001, p. 422) also reviewed three studies presented at scientific conferences suggesting causal relationships between goal orientations and athletes' persistence in sport, but they admitted that more work is needed in this area.

Cross-sectional studies in the USA (e.g. Duda, 1989) and Greece (e.g. Papaioannou, 1997b) have indicated positive relationship between participation in sport and goal orientations, but it is still unclear whether this is the cause or effect of youngsters' involvement in sport. According to social learning theory (Bandura, 1986), participation in sport is expected to cultivate youngsters' goals to further improve and demonstrate their sport abilities. Hence, the positive relationship between goal orientations and participation in sport found in cross-sectional studies could be ascribed to social learning effects of sport involvement on goal orientations, rather than the opposite as suggested by achievement goal theory. Additionally, longitudinal studies examining the causality between goal orientations and physical activity involvement are needed to clarify this issue. In line with achievement goals theory (Elliott & Dweck, 1988; Nicholls, 1984), these studies should also report the interactive effects of ego orientation and perceived competence, which is often omitted in the achievement goal literature. In addition, given the different opinions about the role of ego orientation in sport achievement (Duda, 1997; Hardy, 1997), the interactive effects of task and ego orientation should also are reported. One could hypothesize that the positive effects of task orientation on sport involvement are even stronger when they are accompanied by high ego orientation, but they are undermined when they are joined by low ego orientation (Hardy, 1997), although some authors suggest that ego orientation has no benefit in youth sports (Liukkonen, Telama, & Biddle, 1998). Enjoyment in physical education is linked with adolescents' sport and exercise participation (Sallis et al., 1999; Srucky-Ropp & DiLorenzo, 1993; Zakarian et al., 1994). Across numerous theoretical frameworks, enjoyment is considered an important facet of intrinsically motivated behaviours (e.g. Csikszentmihalyi & Nakamura, 1989; Deci & Ryan, 1985; Harter, 1978; Lepper & Greene, 1978; Nicholls, 1989). Vallerand and Rousseau (2001) suggested that intrinsic motivation is related to behaviours performed due to interest and enjoyment. As has been already mentioned, in all theoretical models perceived competence is deemed an important correlate of positive affect and intrinsic motivation. Indeed, studies in physical activity contexts adopting different theoretical frameworks have concluded that perceived athletic competence is an important determinant of intrinsic motivation (e.g. Chatzisarantis, Hagger, Biddle, Smith, & Wank, 2003; Goudas, Biddle, & Fox, 1994; Lintunen, Valkonen, Leskínen, & Biddle, 1999; Papaíoannou & Theodorakis, 1996; Vallerand & Reid, 1984; Weiss *et al.*, 1986). In line with achievement goals theory (Nicholls, 1989), some of these studies also revealed that both task orientation and perceived athletic competence determine intrinsic motivation (e.g. Goudas *et al.*, 1994; Lintunen *et al.*, 1999; Papaioannou & Theodorakis, 1996).

Given the promotion of physical activity through school physical education, one would expect the causal effects of intrinsic motivation in physical education on participation in physical activity to be clear. However, there has been little relevant robust research. The positive link between physical activity and intrinsic motivation in physical education, which is typically found in cross-sectional studies (e.g. Sallis *et al.*, 1999), may simply reflect the positive effects of out-of-school sport and exercise involvement on intrinsic motivation in physical education. In this study, research examined the causal relationship of intrinsic motivation in physical education with out-of-school participation in sport and exercise.

A 14 month longitudinal questionnaire study, conducted in three waves. First, structural equation models investigating the causal relationship between participation in sport and exercise were constructed and each of the variables pertaining to perceived athletic competence, intrinsic motivation, task and ego orientation, respectively. These analyses show whether each of the cognitive-affective variables is a cause or effect of participation in sport and exercise, irrespective of their relationship with other variables. In these models, the age effects were controlled because task orientation, perceived athletic competence and intrinsic motivation in physical education decline with age (Digelidis & Papaioannou, 1999; Papaioannou, 1997a). Moreover, in line with previous research (Goudas *et al.*, 1994; Lintunen *et al.*, 1999; Papaioannou & Theodorakis, 1996), the effects of perceived competence and task orientation on intrinsic motivation, were examined. More specifically, were investigated whether the effects of perceived competence and task orientation on future sport and exercise behaviour are mediated through intrinsic motivation. Hence, a model was developed that included sport and exercise behaviour, goal orientations, perceived competence and intrinsic motivation, which were assessed three times. Finally, whether the interactions between the two goal orientations, between perceived competence and ego orientation, and between perceived competence and task orientation had any impact on future sport and exercise involvement, were determined.

METHODS

Participants and Procedures

An important complication in this study was the requirement in law (by the Greek Ministry of Education) that all questionnaires should be completed anonymously. Hence, for the purposes of the present study, Time 1, Time 2 and Time 3 cases were matched on the basis of class identification, gender and date of birth. Because not all students provided a proper date of birth on all occasions, many cases could not be matched.

At Time 1 (3-5 weeks into the academic year), nine research assistants administered the questionnaires το 4423 students who were in the fifth (n = 786, age 11± 0.5 years), seventh and eighth (n = 1864), and tenth and eleventh (n = 1773) grades. At Time 2 (3 - 6 weeks before the end of the academic year), the same assistants visited the same classes and administered the questionnaires to 4170 students who were present. Based on these reports, 2414 students could successfully be matched for Time 1 and Time 2 responses. It is important to emphasize that many of the students who apparently had only Time 1 or only Time 2 responses actually had both Time 1 and Time 2 responses but could not be matched on the basis of available data. Seven months after Time 2 (i.e. Time 3), the same research assistants administered the questionnaires to 3641 students who were identified by their teachers as having completed the questionnaires at Times 1 and 2. Students' answers to two items assessing whether they had responded to the questionnaire at Time 1 and Time 2 indicated that 326 had responded at Time 1 only, 567 had responded at Time 2 only, and 2501 had responded at both Time 1 and Time 2 (269 did not complete this item). Based on students' reports on class, gender and date of birth, we matched Time 3 records with the matched records of Time 1 and Time 2. We found records of 882 (329 males, 553 females) students who were successfully matched for Time 1, Time 2 and Time 3 responses.

To ensure that the responses of these 882 students did not differ from the responses of the overall cohort of participants, an attrition analysis was conducted. The scores of the 882 students at Time 1, 2 and 3 were compared with the scores of the remaining students at Time 1, 2 and 3, respectively. For all variables shown below, the differences were largely non-significant. Hence, the following analyses are based on the records of 882 students. At Time 3, these students were in the sixth grade (n = 188), eighth grade (n = 189), ninth grade (n = 208), eleventh grade (n = 141) and twelfth grade (n = 156). They were attending 71 randomly selected (i.e. by lottery) schools from those located in nine different geographical areas of Greece, 67% of them in urban (1.5-4.5 million people) and 33% of them in suburban (50,000 To 70,000 people) areas. Of the 882 students, 35.9% were current athletes (i.e. they were trained in a sport club by a coach) and 64.1 % were not.

Student consent and permission from the Ministry of Education and the school authorities was obtained.

Measures

Task and Ego Orientation in Physical Education Questionnaire (TEOPEQ)

This instrument (Duda & Nicholls, 1992), which is used widely in Greece, has been adapted for physical education classes and has been shown to have very good psychometric properties (e.g. Papaioannou & Macdonald, 1993; Papaioannou & Theodorakis, 1996). Following the stem "I feel most successful in physical education when.. ."), students respond to the seven task-oriented items (e.g. "I learn something that is fun to do") and six ego-oriented items (e.g. "The others can't do as well as me") of the instrument. Students respond to a 5-point Likert scale (5 = *Strongly agree,* 1 = *Strongly disagree).*

Perceived Athletic Competence

This subscale is part of the five-scale physical self-perception profile developed by Fox and Corbin (1989). It consists of six items (e.g. "Some people feel that they are among the best when it comes to athletic ability") and has been used several rimes in Greek physical activity settings and exhibits good psychometric properties (e.g. Digelidis & Papaioannou, 1999). In the present study, the one negatively worded item was excluded because it substantially reduced the internal consistency of the subscale. In line with recent research involving this scale (e.g. Biddle, Soos, & Chatzisarantis, 1999; Lintunen *et al.*, 1999), students responded to a 5-point scale (5 = *Very much like me* To 1 = *Not at all like me*).

Intrinsic Motivation in Physical Education

We used the positively worded items of the enjoyment and effort subscales of the Intrinsic Motivation Inventory (IMI; McAuley, Duncan, & Tammen, 1989) adapted for Greek physical education (Digelidis & Papaioannou, 1999). Existing research indicates a rather weak factor structure of the IMI and four of its five subscales are considered either to be determinants (i.e. perceived competence and perceived locus of causality) or consequences (i.e. effort, pressure-tension) of intrinsic motivation (Markland & Hardy, 1997; Vallerand & Fortier, 1998). On the other hand, Vallerand and Fortier (1998) underscored that the IMI is a flexible instrument and can be readily modified for almost any type of physical activity. Indeed, several researchers have used the IMI in conjunction with the goal orientation and perceived competence measures employed here (e.g. Duda, Chi, Newton, Walling, & Carley, 1995; Lintunen *et al.*, 1999). In addition, previous research suggests that the Greek versions of the enjoyment and effort subscales had good factor structure and internal consistency (Digelidis & Papaioannou, 1999).

Behavior

To assess frequency of sport and exercise, the students were asked how many times during the last month they participated in vigorous sport or exercise outside school physical education. "Vigorous" activity was defined as sport/exercise activity that increases substantially people's heart rates, usually to more than 120 beats. min^{-1}. This activity should last an hour or more in one bout of physical activity. It was explained to the students that this happens when they participate in activities such as basketball, football, swimming and aerobics. Their responses were provided on a 6-point scale *(Not at all,* 1-5, *5-10, 10-15, 15-20* and *Over 20)*. Students were also asked To indicate the average amount of time spent performing sport or exercise on each occasion.

Preliminary Confirmatory Factor Analysis

The current measures are part of a larger investigation and elaborative evidence of their factorial validity is presented elsewhere (H. Marsh, A. Papaioannou, & Y. Theodorakis, unpublished). Briefly, a confirmatory factor analysis was conducted on the larger sample of the marched records of Time 1 and Time 2. This model included the two goal orientation factors, the perceived athletic competence factor, the enjoyment and effort factors, the behaviour factor, age, gender and age X gender, as well as five additional factors irrelevant To the purposes of the current study, assessed at Time 1 and again at Time 2. In roral, 25 factors were inferred on the basis of responses to 95 items. A highly restrictive *a priori* model was constructed, in which each indicator was allowed to load only on the *a priori* factor that it was designed to measure. The findings indicated a very good factor structure, as all factor loadings were highly significant and substantial and the goodness of fit was very good in relation to traditional guidelines (e.g. $\chi^2 = 12298.08$, d.f. = 4030, Tucker-Lewis Index = 0.923, root mean square error of approximation = 0.027).

RESULTS

Times 1, 2 and 3: Causal Relationship of Each Cognitive-affective Variable with Sport and Exercise Involvement

The analysis of longitudinal data at the three times was made using structural equation modelling. A significant advantage of this analysis is that it allows one to examine the assumption that the errors of

measurement associated with one indicator are related to errors of measurement in other indicators. This is particularly important in longitudinal studies in which the same participants complete the same instruments on multiple occasions. According to Joreskog (1979), when responses are given on the same items on multiple occasions, the corresponding residual error variables will tend to be correlated. He also suggested that accurate estimates of relations among constructs could be obtained if correlations among errors are estimated. Hence, correlated uniquenesses were allowed between the same variables at different time points.

Two indicators were used for the latent variable sport and exercise involvement - that is, frequency of sport or exercise and duration per session. This was done because in structural equation modelling it is important to have multiple indicators of each latent variable to model measurement error appropriately. In all measurements, the alpha reliability for the behaviour scale was greater than 0.65. For the latent variables task orientation, ego orientation, intrinsic motivation and perceived athletic competence, the items described in the Methods section were used as indicators. Due to suggestions that enjoyment and effort are not necessarily concomitants, but effort is a consequence of enjoyment and intrinsic motivation (Vallerand & Fortier, 1998). Separate models were computed for effort and enjoyment.

Five models were developed to assess the causal effects between sport and exercise involvement and each of the five cognitive-affective constructs. Each model included two latent variables measured at Time 1, Time 2 and Time 3. One of these latent variables was always sport and exercise involvement and the second was one of the items assessing task orientation, ego orientation, perceived athletic competence, enjoyment and effort in physical education, respectively. The ordering of pairs was strictly based on the temporal ordering of the variables: all Time 1 variables preceded all Time 2 variables and the latter preceded all Time 3 variables. The latent variables of each pair were assumed to affect the latent variables of the next pair. It was also specified that only latent variables assessed at a prior time had effects on subsequent latent variables. Thus, the latent variables of the same pair were correlated at Time 1 but uncorrelated at Times 2 and 3.

The purpose of models 1- 5 was twofold: (1) to examine the psychometric properties of the present instruments and their stability over time, and (2) to investigate the importance of each cognitive-affective variable for adolescents' sport and exercise involvement irrespective of their relationship with other intrapersonal variables. Moreover, for each model, to control for age differences age was added as a correlate of sport and exercise involvement and the respective cognitive-affective variable at Time 1, and as a predictor of sport and exercise involvement and the respective cognitive-affective variable at Time 2. Of particular interest here is the effect of age on sport and exercise involvement and each cognitive-affective variable at Time 2, controlling for age differences in sport and exercise involvement and each cognitive-affective variable at Time 1. This is an alternative to analysis of covariance, allowing measurement error in the covariates (Arbuckle & Wothke, 1999).

Following suggestions by Duncan and Stoolmiller (1993) and Marsh (1989), the appropriate paired uniquenesses or errors to covary were allowed. Taking into consideration the relatively large sample size, the values for χ^2 were expected to be high and, therefore, other indices were also computed. Based on the findings of Marsh and Balla (1994) and Marsh, Balla and Macdonald (1988), the Tucker-Lewis index (TLI) and root mean square error of approximation (RMSEA) were calculated. In addition, the comparative fit index (CFI) (Bentler, 1990) is also provided. The results imply that most models fit the data reasonably well except for model 1, for which the goodness-of-fit indices were relatively low (Hu & Bentler, 1999).

The findings stemming from these structural equation modelling analyses suggested that the latent sport and exercise involvement, task orientation, ego orientation, perceived athletic competence, enjoyment and effort factors were well defined. For example, in the first model, three standardized factor loadings were below 0.50 and none were below 0.38. In the second model, only one standardized factor loading was below 0.50 (0.43); in the third model just one standardized factor loading was below 0.55 (0.43); and in the fourth and fifth models one standardized factor loading was below 0.60 (0.39). All these factor loadings were highly significant.

In line with predictions, age had a negative relationship with sport and exercise involvement at Time 1, implying that older students participate less in sport and exercise than younger students. Moreover, controlling for age differences in sport and exercise involvement at Time 1, significant differences emerged in sport and exercise involvement at Time 2. Additional analysis showed that while participation in sport and exercise increased significantly for elementary school students from Time 1 to Time 2 ($P = 0.002$, $\eta2 = 0.10$), for senior high school students sport and exercise involvement decreased significantly from Time 1 to Time 2 ($P = 0.02$, $\eta2 = 0.02$).

In addition to the four critical paths, the other consistently large paths are stability coefficients - that is, paths connecting the same constructs at different times. These results are important because they suggest that the present measures remained relatively stable over time. This finding supports the reliability of the measures and adds to the robustness of the present research methodology.

Task Orientation and Participation in Sport and Exercise

The path from task orientation at Time 1 to sport and exercise involvement at Time 2 was positive and statistically significant. In other words, task orientation at Time 1 influenced involvement in physical activities 7 months later, beyond the effect of prior involvement in physical activities. Nevertheless, the effect of task orientation at Time 2 on sport and exercise involvement at Time 3 was not significant. Participation in sport and exercise had consistently positive effects on subsequent formation of task orientation beyond the effects of prior task orientation. However, it should be noted that the magnitude of these effects was small. Age was negatively related with task orientation at Time 1 and it had a negative effect on task orientation at Time 2.

Ego Orientation and Participation in Sport and Exercise

Ego orientation had no effect on subsequent participation in sport and exercise. There is inconclusive evidence that prior involvement in physical activities affects subsequent ego orientation. That is, the path from sport and exercise involvement at Time 2 to subsequent ego orientation was positive and statistically significant, but the path from sport and exercise involvement at Time 1 to ego orientation at Time 2 was not statistically significant. Age had no effect on ego orientation at Time 2.

Perceived Athletic Competence and Participation in Sport and Exercise

The four critical paths in model 3 provide clear evidence that the causal effects between sport and exercise involvement and perceived athletic competence are reciprocal. That is, all paths from prior perceived athletic competence to subsequent sport and exercise involvement were statistically significant, and all paths from prior sport and exercise involvement to subsequent perceived athletic competence were significant. Age had a negative association with perceived competence at Time 1 and a negative effect on perceived athletic competence at Time 2.

Enjoyment in Physical Education and Participation in Sport and Exercise

Prior sport and exercise involvement had significant effects on subsequent enjoyment in physical education lessons at both Times 2 and 3. Enjoyment in physical education at Time 1 had significant effects on sport and exercise involvement at Time 2. On the other hand, enjoyment in physical education lessons at Time 2 had no effects on sport and exercise involvement at Time 3. The negative relationship between age and enjoyment at Time 1, as well as the negative impact of age on enjoyment at Time 2, was noticeable.

Effort in Physical Education and Participation in Sport and Exercise

At both Times 1 and 2, prior sport and exercise involvement had a positive effect on subsequent effort in physical education. On the other hand, effort in physical education at Time 1 had a positive effect on sport and exercise involvement at Time 2, but effort at Time 2 had no effect on sport and exercise involvement at Time 3. Age had a negative relationship with effort at Time 1 and at Time 2.

Times 1, 2 and 3: The Full Model

A model was constructed involving all variables measured at all three times. To reduce the number of parameters, the first four task orientation items were combined to form one scale and the remaining three task orientation items were combined to form a second scale (Bandalos & Finney, 2001). These two scales were used as indicators of the latent variable task orientation. Similarly, the first three ego orientation items were combined to form one scale and the remaining three items to form a second scale; these two scales were used as indicators of the ego orientation latent variable. Similarly, the first three perceived athletic ability items were combined to form one scale and the remaining two items to form a second scale; these two scales were used as indicators of the perceived competence latent variable. The effort and enjoyment subscales were used as the two indicators of the intrinsic motivation latent variable (McAuley *et al.,* 1989).

The structure of the model was based on the temporal assessment of the variables. The four cognitive-affective latent variables at Time 1 and the sport and exercise involvement latent variable at Time 1 were used as exogenous variables. Positive relationships between the exogenous variables were predicted. At Times 2 and 3, all latent variables were considered to be endogenous. It was assumed that all exogenous variables had direct effects on sport and exercise involvement at Time 2. In turn, sport and exercise involvement at Time 2 was assumed to have an effect on all cognitive-affective variables at Time 3. Direct paths were also drawn from all Time 2 cognitive affective variables to sport and exercise involvement at Time 3.

Finally, scale scores for perceived competence and task and ego orientation at Times 1 and 2 were computed and centred. Then, for each of Times 1 - 3, the interaction terms between ego orientation and task orientation, ego orientation and perceived competence, and task orientation and perceived competence were computed. These interaction terms were also included in the model - that is, the interaction terms at Time 1 were considered exogenous variables affecting sport and exercise involvement at Time 2, and the interaction terms at Time 2 were considered endogenous variables affecting sport and exercise involvement at Time 2. Because none of these interactions had any significant impact on participation in sport and exercise, for reasons of simplicity these findings are not reported. Given that ego orientation had no effect on subsequent participation in sport and exercise, ego orientation was excluded from the model.

The goodness-of-fit indices for this model suggested a rather good fit of the data. All latent variables were well defined - that is, just one standardized factor loading was below 0.62 (0.45) and all of them were statistically significant (P< 0.001).

All stability coefficients were significant (P < 0.001) and of moderate value (standardized betas greater than 0.40). Intrinsic motivation at Time 1 had direct effects on sport and exercise involvement at Time 2. The path from task orientation at Time 1 to sport and exercise involvement at Time 2 was not significant. This finding suggests that the effects of task orientation at Time 1 on sport and exercise involvement at Time 2 that emerged previously were indirect. Perceived competence had direct effects on sport and exercise involvement both at Time 1 and Time 2. Sport and exercise involvement at Time 2 affected task orientation, intrinsic motivation and perceived competence at both Times 1 and 2.

Times 1 and 3: Cansal Relationship of Each Cognitive-affective Variable with Participation in Sport and Exercise

Intrigued by the non-significant influence of task orientation, enjoyment and effort at Time 2 on sport and exercise involvement at Time 3, we examined whether task orientation and intrinsic motivation at Time 1 had significant effects on sport and exercise involvement at Time 3.

It is important to indicate that the stability coefficients (autocorrelations) between the Time 1 and Time 3 measures remained relatively robust that is, all of them were statistically significant and of moderate value except ego orientation, which was relatively low (beta = 0.33, $P < 0.001$). Most important though are the significant effects of task orientation, enjoyment and effort at Time 1 on participation in sport and exercise at Time 3. These effects were weaker than the effects of Time 1 on Time 2 variables, but this is natural given the longer temporal difference between the measurements. It was also revealed that perceived competence at Time 1 had positive effects on sport and exercise involvement at Time 3. On the other hand, sport and exercise involvement at Time 1 had positive effects on perceived competence, ego orientation, effort and enjoyment at Time 3. Finally, age had noticeable negative effects on sport and exercise involvement as well as on task orientation, effort and enjoyment at Time 3.

DISCUSSION

Research revealing the determinants of physical activity provides an important contribution to public health (Sallis & Owen, 1998). A number of intrapersonal variables are considered important determinants of physical activity in youth, including age, self-efficacy and enjoyment (Sallis & Owen, 1998). In line with existing theories (Deci & Ryan, 1985; Harter, 1978; Nicholls, 1989), the present findings indicate that perceived athletic competence, task orientation and intrinsic motivation in physical education are determinants of participation in sport and exercise in adolescence. Physical education accounts for a large percentage of the physical activity requirements of this age group, particularly in densely populated cities such as in the case of Greece (World Health Organization, 2000). The results of this study suggest that aiming for an increase in task orientation, effort and enjoyment in physical education and perceived athletic competence will enhance youngsters' sport and exercise involvement. Moreover, the present findings imply that ego orientation does not determine sport and exercise involvement in Greece. Hence, trying to increase competition among youngsters does not seem fruitful for the promotion of physical activity in youth.

The present study provides clear support for the positive role of perceived athletic competence in determining future participation in sport and exercise in adolescence. According to all social cognitive theories of motivation (Bandura, 1986; Deci and Ryan, 1985; Harter, 1978; Weiner, 1985), higher perceived ability keeps students' expectations for success high and motivates them to continue their involvement in sport and exercise. The results of this study clearly indicate that policies aimed at promoting sport and exercise in adolescents, showed include strategies reinforcing adolescents' perceived athletic ability. Social learning theory (Bandura, 1986) suggests that modelling and verbal persuasion are important means To enhance youngsters' perceptions of competence. In line with the predictions of social learning theory, this study has shown that involvement in sport activities has positive effects on perceived athletic ability. Hence, actions targeting youth behaviour and not just cognition are also required, such as increased opportunities to participate in sport and exercise. The strict selective system of Greek sport foundations and sport clubs excludes from sport involvement large numbers of youngsters who are not selected as talented individuals. These youngsters find it difficult to find somewhere to take part in physical activity in the densely populated cities of Greece. Thus, comprehensive intervention programmes are required that target changes in perceived athletic competence and other intrapersonal variables as well as social and environmental variables simultaneously.

In line with the predictions of achievement goal theory (Dweck, 1986; Nicholls, 1989), task orientation emerged as an important predictor of involvement in youth sport and exercise (Duda & Hall, 2001). Task orientation is linked with adaptive cognitive-affective motivational patterns, such as intrinsic motivation. The present findings are consistent with theory (e.g. Deci & Ryan, 1985; Nicholls, 1989) and previous research findings (e.g., Goudas *et al.,* 1994; Lintunen *et al., 1999;* Papaioannou & Theodorakis, 1996), suggesting that task orientation and perceived competence determine intrinsic motivation and the latter has a positive impact on physical activity involvement. Hence, policies aimed at fostering both task orientation and intrinsic motivation in physical education should be pursued in the quest to increase participation by youth in physical activity. This can be achieved through the development of a task-involving climate (Ames, 1992) in physical education classes (Papaioannou & Goudas, 1999; Treasure & Roberts, 1995) and the adoption of strategies facilitating self-determination (e.g. Prusak, Treasure, Darst, & Pangrazi, 2004).

Task orientation and intrinsic motivation at Time 1 had a positive impact on physical activity involvement at Time 2 and Time 3. On the other hand, task orientation and intrinsic motivation at Time 2 had no effects on physical activity involvement at Time 3. It should be noted that the Time 1 measures were recorded soon after the begining of the academic year, when teachers' impact on students' task orientation and intrinsic motivation in physical education was still minor, whereas the Time 2 measures were recorded towards the end of the academic year when they were probably affected by teaching. Moreover, in two previous intervention studies in Greek physical education, the impact of teachers on students' task orientation and intrnsic motivation in physical education towards the end of the academic year did not continue for the next 7 months, when the intervention was over and most of the students had new teachers (Christodoulidis, Papaioannou, & Digelidis, 2001; Digelidis, Papaioannou, Christodoulidis, & Laparidis, 2003). Thus, when teachers' effects are not consistent over the years, a substantial part of teachers' impact on task orientation and intrinsic motivation vanishes. Altogether, these findings may imply that task orientation and intrinsic motivation in physical education are better predictors of sport and exercise involvement when they are assessed at the beginning of the academic year, because at that time students' responses are less dependent on temporary contextual influences, and are more likely to reflect differences between individuals that remain relatively stable across time. These differences between students are probably caused by out-of-school social factors, such as family, peers, sport involvement, and so on. It would be interesting to see if future research adopting a similar methodology would produce similar findings.

It is important to stress that task orientation, intrinsic motivation and perceived sport competence at the beginning of the school year predicted participation in sport and exercise 7 and 14 months later. Hence, the effects of these variables last for a considerable time, which implies that attempts to foster them are worthwhile. Nevertheless, if these effects are pursued through school physical education, they should be consistent - that is, they should be sustained across academic years. The implications go beyond the efforts of individual teachers and they mainly concern education policy makers. Attempts to cultivate task orientation and intrinsic motivation in physical education should primarily be reflected in school curricula and school motivational climate (Maehr & Midgley, 1996). The development of a mastery climate should be pursued at school level and the promotion of task orientation should be a priority of the educational system. This will ensure that the positive influence of teachers will be carried on by their successors in the following years. Only then can we expect positive teaching effects to remain constant across time.

The adjustment of age effects on sport and exercise involvement should be considered a strength of this study. Most studies in the sport motivation literature did not control for age differences. Nevertheless, this study provides support for past research (Papaioannou, 1997a; Digelidis and Papaioannou, 1999) suggesting that there is a considerable reduction in youngsters' motivation in physical education with age. Furthermore, this study showed that during an academic year age had a negative impact on physical activity involvement as well as on task orientation, intrinsic motivation in physical education and perceived athletic competence (Maehr & Midgley, 1996). The loss of motivation in physical activity contexts was more obvious for older Greek students. One might ascribe this to the enhanced interest of older students in a variety of activities that conflicts with their interest in sport and exercise. Nevertheless, this is a rather naive explanation. Recent research indicates that older adolescents are more likely to consider athletic ability as a fixed entity than younger adolescents and elementary school children (Xiang, Lee, & Williamson, 2001). This has unfortunate consequences for adolescents' motivation in physical activity contexts because they develop a helpless approach with regard to physical ability development (Dweck, 1986). The climate in youth physical activity settings should help adolescents believe that physical ability is a malleable quality that is primarily dependent on effort (Ommundsen, 2001). This will boost their expectations to increase physical competence with practice. At the same time, a mastery environment should be established in school physical education as well as in youth sport and exercise settings. Students should be assisted to set personal goals and to commit themselves to these goals, while at the same time retaining a sense of self-determination (Papaioannou & Goudas, 1999; Treasure & Roberts, 1995).

While task orientation was a determinant of sport and exercise involvement, ego orientation was not. Neither ego orientation at Time 1 nor ego orientation at Time 2 had any effect on subsequent participation in sport and exercise. It is possible that the relationship between ego orientation and participation in sport and exercise that emerged in the cross-secrional data, such as at Time 1 ($r = 0.19$, $P < 0.001$), Time 2 ($r = 0.18$, $P < 0.001$) and Time 3 ($r = 0.13$, $P < 0.001$), reflected the effect of the competitive nature of youth sport on youngsters' goal to show their ability. These findings indicate that adolescents' involvement in sport and exercise affected their perceived athletic competence and this had a temporary impact on their goal to show their ability. However, this effect was not sustained. There was live evidence of a substantial impact of sport and exercise involvement on ego orientation 7 months later. In summary, these results imply that for the Greek students in this study, ego orientation was not a cause but a temporary effect of sport and exercise involvement.

Contrary to theoretical predictions (Nicholls, 1984), we found no evidence of motivational benefits due to an interaction of ego orientation with perceived competence. In a similar vein, the interaction of ego orientation with task orientation had no effect on sport and exercise involvement and intrinsic motivation in physical education. Recently, Grant and Dweck (2003) suggested that for ego involved individuals focusing primarily on normative comparisons, the motivational consequences are different than for ego-involved persons who primarily strive to validate their ability. The present measure of ego orientation incorporated normative but not ability goal items; however, it is possible that there will be an interaction between perceived competence and a scale including ability goal items. The effects of the interaction of ego orientation with perceived competence and task orientation should be examined in further research. Also, longitudinal and field experimental studies are needed. Findings from laboratory studies (e.g. Elliott & Dweck, 1988) offer a very limited picture of the psychological processes that occur in the complex social environment. Moreover, many statistically significant results revealed by cross-sectional studies (e.g. Duda, 1989) are not sustained for long, an outcome that emerged repeatedly in this study. The results of this study offer little encouragement to those who favor an ego orientation in youth sport and exercise contexts. Taking the present findings in combination with the negative effects of ego orientation on social behavior (e.g. Duda, Olson, & Templin, 1991; Papaioannou, 1997b), the implication for parents and coaches is to lower their emphasis on ego orientation in sport.

One limitation of this study was the large proportion of students who participated in the study but were not matched for Time 1, Time 2 and Time 3 responses. The attrition analysis did not reveal any difference between these students and the 882 students whose data were used here. Hence, we have no idea of knowing whether this decrease in sample size may have influenced the results. Another limitation of the study is concerned with the measurement of behavior that incorporated both sport and exercise involvement. Although this measure is more ecologically relevant on terms of adolescents' involvement in physical activity settings than a measure focusing solely on either sport or exercise settings, it should be acknowledged that predictions based on achievements goal theory are primarily concerned with sport involvement because sport is an achievement setting. The percentage of Greek adolescents who select competitive sport as their main form of physical activity is substantially higher than the percentage of youngsters who prefer other forms of exercise (Papaioannou, Karastogiannidou, & Theodorakis, 2004) and this may have influenced the results of the present study. Hence, the present conclusions cannot be applied to youngsters who are primarily involved in non-competitive exercise settings and, therefore, further research is needed in this area.

Although we did not focus on measurement issues here, it is important to note that the present instruments exhibited very good psychometric properties. Of particular interest are the moderate stability coefficients for both behavioral and cognitive-affective constructs. Hertzog and Nesselroade (1987) suggested that the magnitude of the stability coefficient can be interpreted as high or low depending upon psychometric concerns and theoretical expectations. The test - retest results presented here are in line with expectations (e.g. Duda & Whitehead, 1998; Fox, 1998). The magnitude of the stability coefficients for the goal orientation variables over a 7 month period was not substantially lower than the magnitude of the test-retest correlation coefficients reported by Duda and Whitehead (1998) for a 3 week period. The magnitude of the test retest correlation coefficients for the perceived athletic competence scale over a 23 day period (Fox, 1998) was higher than the magnitude of the present stability coefficients, but this should be expected given the longer time interval in the current study. These findings support the reliability of the present measures. In addition, they indicate that the change of sport and exercise involvement, task orientation, perceived competence and intrinsic motivation over 7 and 14 months was noteworthy. This is in line with theories of achievement goals (Nicholls, 1989), intrinsic motivation (e.g. Deci & Ryan, 1985) and effectance motivation (Harter, 1978) that predict a substantial impact of social factors on these social-cognitive variables. This is good news for individuals who wish to intervene using these variables, because there is significant room for their improvement.

Table 1. Structural equation models investigating the effects of Time 1 variable on Time 3 variables

Paths	Standardized beta	Goodness-of-fit indices
Model 1: Task orientation and SEI		
SEI-1 → Task-3	0.04	$\chi^2 = 391$
Task-1 → SEI-3	0.10**	d.f. = 121
Task-1 → Task-3	0.46***	TLI = 0.915
SEI-1 → SEI-3	0.43***	CFI = 0.929
Age → Task-3	− 0.19***	RMSEA = 0.050
Age → SEI-3	−0.27***	
Model 2: Ego orientation and SEI		
SEI-1 → Ego-3	0.13***	$\chi^2 = 382$
Ego-1 → SEI-3	0.02	d.f. = 99
Ego-1 → Ego-3	0.33***	TLI = 0.931
SEI-1 → SEI-3	0.41***	CFI = 0.943
Age → Ego-3	0.00	RMSEA = 0.057
Age → SEI-3	−0.33***	
Model 3: Perceived competence and SEI		
SEI-1 → PC-3	0.15***	$\chi^2 = 246$
PC-1 → SEI-3	0.17***	d.f. = 72
PC-1 → PC-3	0.43***	TLI = 0.939
SEI-1 → SEI-3	0.37***	CFI = 0.952
Age → PC-3	−0.06	RMSEA = 0.052
Age → SEI-3	−0.28***	
Model 4: Enjoyment and SEI		
SEI-1 → Enjoyment-3	0.10**	$\chi^2 = 84$
Enjoyment-1 → SEI-3	0.13***	d.f. = 30
Enjoyment-1 → Enjoyment-3	0.42***	TLI = 0.981
SEI-1 → SEI-3	0.38***	CFI = 0.987
Age → Enjoyment-3	−0.24***	RMSEA = 0.045
Age → SEI-3	−0.28***	
Model 5: Effort and SEI		
SEI-1 → Effort-3	0.10**	$\chi^2 = 131$
Effort-1 → SEI-3	0.16**	d.f. = 30
Effort-1 → Effort-3	0.48***	TLI = 0.959
SEI-1 → SEI-3	0.39***	CFI = 0.973
Age → Effort-3	−0.26***	RMSEA = 0.045
Age → SEI-3	−0.26***	

SEI = sport and exercise involvement; PC = perceived athletic competence; d.f. = degrees of freedom; TLI = Tucker-Lewis index; CFI = comparative fit index; RMSEA = root mean square error of approximation.

* P < 0.05, *** P < 0.001.

The results of this study support the positive role of perceived athletic competence, task orientation and intrinsic motivation in physical education for sport and exercise involvement. Further studies examining the mediator variables between sport and exercise involvement and task orientation, perceived competence and intrinsic motivation are called for. It is important to understand the self regulation strategies adopted by youngsters who are highly task-oriented and high in perceived competence that trigger their sport and exercise behavior. Another research avenue should focus on the social factors affecting students' goal orientations and perceived athletic competence. Interventions on motivational climate in physical education are few and far between (e.g. Christodoulidis *et al.*, 2001; Digelidis *et al.*,

2003; Jaakkola, Kokkonen, & Papaioannou, 2001; Kokkonen, Jaakkola, & Papaioannou, 2001) and further research is needed regarding teaching strategies that cultivate task orientation and intrinsic motivation in physical education (e.g. Goudas, Biddle, Fox, & Underwood, 1995). Finally, the causal relationship of sport and exercise involvement with goal orientations, perceived competence and intrinsic motivation must be investigated in different cultures to determine whether these social-cognitive variables have universal importance. Taking into consideration the importance of physical activity in public health (Bouchard *et al., 1994),* the study of motivation in physical activity settings is more crucial and challenging than ever before.

ACKNOWLEDGEMENTS

The research reported in this paper was financed by the Centre of Educational Research, Greek Ministry of Education. The authors are grateful to Joan Duda and Ken Fox for their valuable insights and to Nikolaos Perkos, Petros Natsis, Eirini Douma, Kalliopi Plessa, Nikolaos Mouzakidis and Argiris Theodosiou for their help with data collection.

REFERENCES

Ames, C. (1992). Classroom goals, structures, and student motivation. *Journal of Educational Psychology,* 84, 261-271.

Arbuckle, J. L, & Wothke, W. (1999). *Amos 4.0: User's guide.* Chicago, IL: SmallWaters Corporation.

Bandalos, D. L, & Finney, S. J. (2001). Item parceling issues in structural equation modeling. In G. A. Marcoulides & R E. Schumaker (Eds.), *New developments and techniques in structural equation modeling* (pp. 269-296). Mahwah, NJ: Lawrence Erlbaum.

Bandura, A. (1986). *Social foundations of thought and action: A social cognitive theory.* Englewood Cliffs, NJ: Prentice-Hall.

Bentler, P.M. (1990). Comparative fix indexes in structural models. *Psychological Bulletin, 107, 238-246.*

Biddle, S., Sallis, J. F., & Cavill, N. A. (Eds.) (1998). *Young and active? Young people and health enhancing physical activity: Evidence and implications.* London: Health Education Authority.

Biddle, S. J .H., Soos, I., & Chatzisarantis, N. (1999). Predicting physical activity intentions using a goal perspectives approach: A study of Finish youth. *Scandinavian Journal of Medicine and Science in Sports,* 9,353-357.

Bouchard, C., Shephard, R., & Stephens, T. (1994). Consensus statement In C. Bouchard, R. Shephard, & T. Stephens (Eds.), *Physical activity, fitness, and health: International proceedings and consensus statement* - (pp. 9-76). Champaign, IL: Human Kinetics.

Chatzisarantis, N., Hagger, M., Biddle, S., Smith, B., & Wank, C. K. (2003). A meta-analysis of perceived locus of causality in exercise, sport, and physical education contexts. *Journal of Sport and Exercise Psychology,* 25, 284 - 306.

Christodoulidis, T., Papaioannou, A., & Digelidis, N. (2001). Motivational climate and attitudes towards exercise in Greek senior high school: A year-long intervention. *European journal of Sport Science,* 1(4), 000-000.

Csikszentmihalyi, M., & Nakamura, J. (1989). The dynamics of intrinsic motivation: A study of adolescents. In C. Ames & R. Ames (Eds.), *Motivation* in *education: Goals and cognitions* (Vol. 3, pp. 45-71). New York: Academic Press.

Deci, E. L, & Ryan, R. M. (1985). *Intrinsic motivation and self determination* in *human behavior.* New York: Plenum Press.

Digelidis, N., & Papaioannou, A. (1999). Age-group differences in intrinsic motivation, goal orientations and perceptions of athletic competence, physical appearance and motivational climate in Greek physical education. *Scandinavian Journal of Medicine and Science in Sports,* 9, 375-380.

Digelidis, N., Papaioannou, A., Christodoulidis, T., & Laparidis, K. (2003). A one-year intervention in 7th grade physical education classes aiming to change motivational climate and attitudes towards exercise. *Psychology of Sport and Exercise, 4,* 195-210.

Duda, J. L (1989). Goal perspectives, participation and persistence in sport. *International Journal of Sport Psychology, 20,* 42 - 56.

Duda, J. L (1997). Perpetuating myths: A response to Hardy's 1996 Coleman Griffith Address. *Journal of Applied Sport Psychology,* 9, 307 - 313.

Duda, J. L (2001). Achievement goal research in sport: Pushing the boundaries and clarifyng some misunderstandings. In G. C. Roberts (Ed.), *Advances* in *motivation* in *sport and exercise* (pp. 129-182). Champaign, IL.: Human Kinetics.

Duda, J., & Hall, H. (2001). Achievement goal theory in sport: Recent extensions and future directions. In R Singer, H. A. Hausenblas, & C. M. Janelle (Eds.), *Handbook of sport psychology* (pp. 417 -443). New York: Wiley.

Duda, J. L, & Nicholls, J. G. (I 992). Dimensions of achievement motivation in schoolwork and sport. *Journal of Educational Psychology,* 84, 290-299.

Duda, J. L., & Whitehead, J. (1998). Measurement of goal perspectives in the physical domain. In J. Duda (Ed.), *Advances in sport and exercise psychology measurement* (pp. 21-48). Morgantown, WV: Fitness Information Technology.

Duda, J. L., Chi, L., Newton, M. L., Walling, M. D., & Catley, D. (1995). Task and ego orientation and intrinsic motivation in sport. *International Journal of Sport Psychology,* 26, 40 - 63.

Duda, J. L., Olson, L. K, & Templin, T. J. (1991). The relationship of task and ego orientation to sportsmanship attitudes and the perceived legitimacy of injurious acts. *Research Quarterly for Exercise and Sport,* 62, 79 - 87.

Duncan, T. E., & Stoolmiller, M. (1993). Modeling social and psychological determinants of exercise behaviors via structural equation systems. *Research Quarterly for Exercise and Sport, 64,* 1-16.

Dweck, C. S. (1986). Motivation processes affecting learning. *American Psychologist,* 41,1040 -1048.

Elliott, A. J., & Church, M. A. (1997). A hierarchical model approach and avoidance achievement motivation. *Journal of Personality and Social Psychology,* 72, 218 - 232.

Elliott, E. S., & Dweck, C. S. (1988). Goals: An approach to motivation and achievement. *Journal of Personality and Social Psychology,* 54, 5 - 12.

Fox, K R. (1998). Advances in the measurement of the physical self. In J. Duda (Ed.), *Advances in sport and exercise psychology measurement* (pp. 295-310). Morgantown, WV: Fitness Information Technology.

Fox, K R, & Corbin, C. B. (1989). The physical self-perception profile: Development and preliminary validation. *Journal of Sport and Exercise Psychology,* 11 (4), 408 - 430.

Fox, K R., Goudas, M., Biddle, S., Duda, J., & Armstrong, N. (1994). Children's task and ego goal profiles in sport. *British Journal of Educational Psychology,* 64, 253 - 261.

Goudas, M., Biddle, S., & Fox, K (1994). Perceived locus of causality, goal orientations, and perceived competence in school physical education classes. *British Journal of Educational Psychology,* 64, 453-463.

Goudas, M., Biddle, S., Fox, K, & Underwood, M. (1995). It ain't what you do, it's the way that you do it. Teaching styles affect children's motivation in track and field lessons. *The Sport Psychologist,* 9, 254 - 264.

Grant, H., & Dweck, C. S. (2003). Clarifying achievement goals and their impact. *Journal of Personality and Social Psychology, 85,* 541 - 553.

Hagger, M. S., Chatzisarantis, N., Culverhouse, T., & Biddle, S. J. H. (2003). The processes by which perceived autonomy support in physical education promotes leisure-time physical activity intentions and behavior: A trans-contextual model. *Journal of Educational Psychology,* 93, 784-795.

Hardy, L. (1997). Three myths about applied consultancy work. *Journal of Applied Sport Psychology,* 9, 277 - 294.

Harter, S. (1978). Effectance motivation reconsidered: Toward a developmental model. *Human Development,* 21,34 - 64.

Hertzog, C., & Nesselroade, J. R. (1987). Beyond autoregressive models: Some implications of the trait-state distinction for the structural modeling of developmental change. *Child Development,* 58, 93 - 109.

Hu, L., & Bentler, P. M. (1999). Cutoff criteria for fit indexes in covariance structure analysis: Conventional criteria versus new alternatives. *Srtuctural Equation Modeling,* 6, 1 - 55.

Jaakkola, T., Kokkonen, J., & Papaioannou, A. (2001). Changes in pupils' goal orientations through an intervention in motivational climate in physical education. In A. Papaioannou, M. Goudas, & Y. Theodorakis (Eds.), *Proceedings of the 10th World Congress of Sport Psychology* (pp. 196-199). TOWN: PUBLISHER.

Joreskog, K G. (1979). Statistical estimation of structural models in longitudinal investigations. In J. R Nesselroade & B. Baltes (Eds.), *Longitudinal research in the study of behavior and development* (pp. 303-351). New York: Academic Press.

Kokkonen, J., Jaakkola, T., & Papaioannou, A. (2001). Changes in motivational climare of PE lessons through one-year intervention. In A. Papaioannou, M. Goudas, & Y. Theodorakis (Eds.), *Proceedings of the 10th World Congress of Sport Psychology* (pp.198-199). TOWN: PUBLISHER.

Lepper, M.R., & Greene, D. (1978). Overjustification research and beyond: Towards a means-ends analysis of intrinsic and extrinsic motivation. In M. R Lepper & D. Greene (Eds.), *The hidden costs of reward: New perspectives on the psychology of human motivation* (pp. 109-148). Hillsdale, NJ: Lawrence Erlbaum.

Lintunen, A., Valkonen, E., Leskinen, E., & Biddle, S. J. H. (1999). Predicting physical activity interventions using a goal perspectives approach: A study of Finnish youth. *Scandinavian Journal of Medicine and Science in Sports, 9*, 344 - 352.

Liukkonen, J., Telama, R., & Biddle, S. (1998). Enjoyment in youth sports: A goal perspectives approach. *European Y earbook of Sport Psychology, 2*, 55 - 75.

Maehr, M. L. (1989). Thoughts about motivation. In C. Ames & R. Ames (Eds.), *Research on motivation in education* (Vol. 3, pp. 299-315). New York: Academic Press.

Maehr, M. L., & Midgley, C. (1996). *Transforming school cultures.* Boulder, CO: Westview Press.

Maehr, M. L., & Nicholls, J. (1980). Culture and achievement motivation: A second look. In N. Warren (Ed.), *Studies in cross culture psychology* (pp. 221-267). New York: Academic Press.

Markland, D., & Hardy, L. (1997). On the factorial and construct validity of the intrinsic motivation inventory: Conceptual and operational concepts. *Research Quarterly for Exercise and Sport,*

68, 20-32.

Marsh, H. W. (1989). Confirmatory factor analyses of multitrait-multimethod data: Many problems and a few solutions. *Applied Psychological Measurement, 13*, 335 - 361.

Marsh, H. W., & Balla, J. (1994). Goodness of fit in confirmatory factor analysis: The effects of sample size and model parsimony. *Quality anode Quantity: International Journal of Methodology, 28*, 185-217.

Marsh, H. W., Balla, J. R., & Macdonald, R. P. (1988). Goodness of-fit indexes in confirmatory factor analysis: The effect of sample size. *Psychological Bulletin, 103*(3), 391 - 410.

McAuley, E., Duncan, T., & Tammen, V. V. (1989). Psychometric properties of the intrinsic motivation inventory in a competitive sport setting: A confirmatory factor analysis. *Research Quarterly for Exercise and Sport, 60*, 48 - 58.

Nicholls, J. G. (1984). Conceptions of ability and achievement motivation. In R. Ames & C. Ames (Eds.), *Research on motivation in education: Vol. 1. Student motivation* (pp. 39 - - 73). New York: Academic Press.

Nicholls, J. G. (1989). *The competitive ethos and democratic education.* Cambridge, MA: Harvard University Press.

Nroumanis, N., & Biddle, S. J. H. (1999). Affect and achievement goals in physical activity: A meta-analysis. *Scandinavian Journal of Medicine and Science in Sports, 9*, 315 - 332.

Ommundsen, Y. (2001). Students' implicit theories of ability in physical education classes: The influence of motivational aspects of the learning environment. *Learning Environments Research, 42*, 139 - 158.

Papaioannou, A. (1997a). Perception of motivational climate, perceived competence, and motivation of students of varying age and sport experience. *Perceptual and Motor Skills, 85*, 419 - 430.

Papaioannou, A. (1997b). "I agree with the referee's abuse, that's how I also beat.. .": Prediction of sport violence and attitudes towards sport violence. *European Yearbook of Sport Psychology, 1*, 113 - 129.

Papaioannou, A., & Goudas, M. (1999). Motivational climate in physical education. In Y. Vanden Auweele, F. Bakker, S. Biddle, M. Durand, & R Seiler (Eds.), *Textbook: Psychology for physical education.* (pp. 51- 68). Champaign, IL.: Human Kinetics.

Papaioannou, A., Karastogiannidou, C., & Theodorakis, Y. (2004). Sport involvement, sport violence and health behaviours of Greek adolescents. *European Journal of Public Health, 14*,168-172.

Papaioannou, A., & Macdonald, A. (1993). Goal perspectives and purposes of physical education among Greek adolescents. *Physical Education Review, 16*, 41 - 48.

Papaioannou, A., & Theodorakis, Y. (1996). A test of three models for the prediction of intention in participation in physical education lessons. *International Journal of Sport Psychology, 27*, 383 - 399.

Prusak, K. A., Treasure, D. C., Darst, P. W., & Pangrazi, P. (2004). The effects of choice on the motivation of adolescent girls in physical education. *Journal of Teaching in Physical Education, 23*, 19 - 29.

Reynolds, K. D., Killen, I. D, Bryson, S. W. *et al. (1990).* Psychosocial predictors of physical activity in adolescents. *Preventive Medicine, 19*, 541-551.

Roberts, G. C. (2001). *Advances in motivation in sport and exercise.* Champaign, IL.: Human Kinetics.

Sallis, I. F., & Owen, N. (1998). *Physical activity and behavioralmedicine.* Thousand Oaks, CA: Sage.

Sallis, I. F., Prochaska, I. I., Taylor, W. C., Hill, I. O., & Geraci, I. C. (1999). Correlates of physical activity in a national sample of girls and boys in grades 4 through 12. *Health Psychology, 18*, 410 - 415.

Sallis, I. F., Simons-Morton, B. G., Stone, E. I. *et al. (1992).* Determinants of physical activity and intervention in youth. *Medicine and Science in Sports and Exercise, 24*, S248 - S257.

Stucky-Ropp, R. C., & DiLorenzo, T. M. (1993). Determinants of exercise in children. *Preventive Medicine, 22*, 880 - 889.

Tappe, M κ., Duda, I. L, & Ehrnwald, P. M. (1989). Perceived barriers of exercise among adolescents. *Journal of School Health, 59*,153 - 155.

Treasure, D., & Roberts, G. (1995). Applications of achievement goal theory to physical education: Implications for enhancing motivation. *Quest, 47*, 475 - 489.

Trost, S. G., Pate, R. R, Saunders, R. *et al.* (1997). A prospective study of the determinants of physical activity in rural fifth-grade children. *Preventive Medicine, 26*, 257 - 263.

Vallerand, R I., & Fortier, M.S. (1998). Measures of intrinsic and extrinsic motivation in sport and physical activity: A review and critique. In I. Duda (Ed.), Advances in *sport and exercise measurement* (pp. 81-104). Morgantown, WV: Fitness Information Technology.

Vallerand, R I., & Reid, G. (1984). On the causal effects of perceived competence on intrinsic motivation: A test of cognitive evaluation theory. *Journal of Sport and Exercise Psychology, 6*, 94 -102.

Vallerand, R I., & Rousseau, F. L (2001). Intrinsic and extrinsic motivation in sport and exercise: A review using the hierarchical model of intrinsic and extrinsic motivation. In R. Singer, H. A. Hausenblas, & C. M. Janelle (Eds.), *Handbook of sport psychology* (pp. 389-416). New York: Wiley.

Weiner, B. (1985). An attributional theory of achievement motivation and emotion. *Psychological Review, 92*, 548 - 573.

Weiss, M. R, Bredemeier, B. I., & Shewchuk, R. M. (1986). The dynamics of perceived competence, perceived control, and motivational orientation in youth sports. In M. R.

Weiss & D. Gould (Eds.), *Sport for children and youths* (pp. 89-101). Champaign, IL.: Human Kinetics.

World Health Organization (2000). *Health and health behaviour among young people.* Geneva: WHO.

Xiang, P., Lce, A., & Williamson, L. (2001). Conceptions of ability in physical education: Children and adolescents. *Journal of Teaching in Physical Education, 20,* 282 - 294.

Zakarian, I. M., Hovell, M. F., Hofstetter, C. R., Sallis, J. F., & Keating, K. I. (1994). Correlates of vigorous exercise in a predominantly low SES high school population. *Preventive Medicine,* 23, 314 - 321.

In: Motivation of Exercise and Physical Activity
Editor: Liam A. Chiang, pp. 35-52

ISBN: 978-1-60021-596-4
© 2007 Nova Science Publishers, Inc.

Chapter 3

WHAT ROLE DOES PSYCHOLOGICAL NEED SATISFACTION PLAY IN MOTIVATING EXERCISE PARTICIPATION?

Philip M. Wilson[*], *Diane E. Mack,* *Sovoeun Muon and Meghan E. LeBlanc*

Faculty of Applied Health Sciences, Brock University, St. Catharines, Ontario, Canada

ABSTRACT

The purpose of this study was to examine Vallerand's (2001) contention that perceptions of psychological need satisfaction underpin the endorsement of different motives, which in turn, predicts behavioural intentions in the context of exercise. Participants (N = 176; 51.2% female) involved in a group-based intramural event completed a self-administered cross-sectional survey comprised of demographic questions, the Psychological Need Satisfaction in Exercise Scale (PNSE; Wilson et al., 2006), the Behavioural Regulation in Exercise Questionnaire (BREQ; Mullan et al., 1997), and a behavioural intention scale (Courneya & McAuley, 1993). Bivariate correlations indicated stronger relationships between fulfillment of the psychological needs for competence, autonomy, and relatedness with identified and intrinsic regulations (r's ranged from 0.47 to 0.67) compared to external and introjected regulations (r's ranged from -0.30 to 0.19). Multivariate analysis using structural equation modeling supported the tenability of a model explaining behavioural intentions (R^2 = 0.17) as a function of a person's relative autonomy motivational index (γ = 41) which in turn was predicted by perceived competence (γ = 0.25), autonomy (γ = 0.53), and relatedness (γ = -0.12) in exercise contexts (χ^2 = 399.47; df = 183; *CFI* = 0.92; *IFI* = 0.92; *RMSEA*

[*] Correspondence concerning this manuscript can be sent to: Philip M. Wilson, Ph.D., Department of Physical Education & Kinesiology, Faculty of Applied Health Sciences, Brock University, 500 Glenridge Avenue, St. Catharines, Ontario, L2S 3A1, Canada. Tel: (905) 688-5550 Ext. 4997. Fax: (905) 688-8364. Email: phwilson@brocku.ca

= 0.08 [90% *CI* = 0.07 to 0.10]). Overall, the results of the present investigation partially support Vallerand's argument regarding the sequences that shape motivational processes in exercise contexts. Furthermore, the results of the present investigation provide support for the importance of psychological need satisfaction for internalized motivation in an applied context which is in line with more general arguments set forth within the framework of self-determination theory (Deci & Ryan, 1985; 2002).

Keywords: construct validity, basic psychological needs subtheory, physical activity

It is well documented that physical activity reduces all-cause mortality and morbidity (Bouchard, Blair, & Haskell, 2007) while enhancing quality of life in various populations (Biddle, Fox, & Boutcher, 2000). Given the importance of physical activity to health promotion, it is surprising that over half (51.0%) of the Canadian population remain inactive (Cameron, Craig, & Paolin, 2005). Complimenting these trends, previous research notes high attrition rates from structured involvement in exercise within 6 months of initial adoption (Craig, Cameron, Russell, & Beaulieu, 2001). Considering the contribution of regular physical activity to population health goals, it seems clear that research examining the reasons why people sustain engagement in physical activity is important. Towards this end, theory-based research addressing participation issues in physical activity has been advocated (Bauman, Sallis, Dzewaltowski, & Owen, 2002; Biddle, Fox, & Boutcher, 2000). One theoretical framework that may be useful for understanding physical activity motivation is self-determination theory (SDT; Deci & Ryan, 2002).

According to Deci and Ryan (2002), motivation lies on a continuum marking distinct regulatory structures responsible for motivating behaviour. The distal ends of the continuum are anchored by amotivation which concerns a lack of intentionality to perform the behaviour or passive compliance, and intrinsic motivation which posits that interest, enjoyment, and novel curiosity regulate behaviour (Deci & Ryan, 2002). Ryan (1995) notes, however, that not all behaviours are amenable to intrinsic motivation and therefore SDT has developed a differentiated approach to extrinsic motivation. At one end of the continuum, extrinsic motives control behaviour through a desire to maximize rewards and avoid punishments (external regulation; Deci & Ryan, 2002) or coerce task persistence through their desire to avoid negative feelings such as guilt or maintain contingent self-worth (introjected regulation; Deci & Ryan, 2002). By contrast, more autonomous processes characterize motivation at the other end of the continuum whereby behaviour is regulated by personal values (identified regulation; Deci & Ryan, 2002) or congruence between a person's identity and the behaviour itself (integrated regulation; Deci & Ryan, 2002). Emerging evidence supports the distinction between these motivational structures in exercise (Mullan, Markland, & Ingledew, 1997) and indicates that autonomous motives predict adaptive consequences including positive self-perceptions (Wilson & Rodgers, 2002), habitual exercise patterns (Mullan & Markland, 1997), and reduced likelihood of exercise dependence (Edmunds, Ntoumanis, & Duda, 2006).

One aspect of SDT that holds considerable appeal for understanding physical activity behaviour is the proposition that basic psychological needs serve as a unifying framework for understanding motivational processes and their impact on health and well-being (Deci & Ryan, 1985; 2002; Ryan 1995). Deci and Ryan (2002) have advocated that basic psychological needs within SDT act as synergistic "nutriments" (p.7) within and across contexts to foster integrative tendencies such as adaptation and adjustment (Ryan, 1995). While other theories equate psychological needs with any desire or drive (Deci & Vansteenkiste, 2004), the view embraced within SDT is that psychological needs are separate from motives and represent the foundation upon which motivational development is either optimized or forestalled (Deci & Ryan, 2002; Ryan, 1995).

Deci and Ryan (1985; 2002) proposed that the psychological needs for competence, autonomy, and relatedness promote the internalization of social norms and values including the regulatory structures motivating behaviour and impacting well-being. Competence refers to interacting effectively within one's environment while mastering challenging tasks or expressing one's capacities (White, 1959). Autonomy involves feeling a sense of personal agency or volition such that one's behaviour is perceived to emanate from an internal locus of causality as opposed to feeling controlled by external agendas (deCharms, 1968). Finally, relatedness involves feeling a meaningful connection to important others within one's social milieu that is characterized by nurturing social relationships or a sense of belongingness to others embedded within a broader community (Baumeister & Leary, 1995).

While the number and function of basic psychological needs remains controversial (Schwartz, 2000), this aspect of SDT has practical appeal given the ability of psychological needs to explain a broad spectrum of human functioning (Deci & Ryan, 2002; Sheldon, Elliot, Kim, & Kasser, 2001) while offering targets for intervention to illicit behavioural or psychological change (Sheldon, Williams, & Joiner, 2003). Research in exercise settings has consistently supported the importance of perceived competence in terms of shaping motivation and subsequent behaviour (Roberts, 2001), and to a lesser extent, a factor impacting well-being (Frederick & Ryan, 1993). However, investigations examining Deci and Ryan's (2002) contentions regarding the link between satisfying autonomy and relatedness needs and exercise motivation has yielded mixed results (Edmunds et al., 2006; Vlachopoulos & Michailidou, 2006; Wilson, Rodgers, Blanchard, & Gessell, 2003). For example, Edmunds et al. (2006) note that only perceived competence predicted intrinsic motivation in British exercisers while Vlachopoulos and Michailidou (2006) report no relationship between perceived autonomy and relatedness with indices of motivation in Greek exercisers. Furthermore, Wilson et al. (2003) reported no meaningful relationship (r's range from .01 to .19; all p's > 0.05) between perceived relatedness and any point along SDT's motivation continuum in a sample of Canadian exercisers.

Considering the importance of basic psychological needs to SDT-based views on motivation, it is difficult to reconcile the aberrant results of investigations conducted in exercise contexts. One plausible explanation for these observations concerns the difficulty of measuring psychological need satisfaction in general (Sheldon, 2002) and in exercise contexts in particular (Wilson et al., 2003). Previous investigations have modified instruments designed to measure psychological need satisfaction in work (Edmunds et al., 2006) or education (Wilson et al., 2003) contexts which may account for the troublesome score reliability evidence observed in these studies (Cronbach's α's ranged from 0.53 to 0.65 respectively) and attenuate the relationship between psychological need satisfaction and exercise motivation. Ryan (1995) has emphasized the importance of domain-specific investigations to determine the degree to which basic principles advanced within SDT generalize across contexts where idiosyncrasies likely impact motivation. Extrapolating from Ryan's (1995) contentions, and previous exercise-based studies, Wilson and colleagues have developed the Psychological Need Satisfaction in Exercise Scale (PNSE; Wilson, Rogers,

Rodgers, & Wild, 2006) as a domain-specific instrument capturing variability in the fulfillment of competence, autonomy, and relatedness needs within exercise settings. Adopting a construct validation approach (Messick 1995), Wilson et al. (2006) provided evidence supporting the structural and convergent validity, as well as, the internal consistency reliability of PNSE subscale scores in a sample of active Canadian exercisers. However, no attempt was made to link PNSE constructs with exercise motives or other variables implied within SDT's nomological network (Cronbach & Meehl, 1955) to determine the manner in which PNSE scores corroborate Deci and Ryan's (2002) arguments concerning the function of psychological needs within SDT.

The overall purpose of this study was to examine the relationship between perceptions of competence, autonomy, and relatedness in exercise settings with exercise motives and behavioural intentions to continue exercising. A secondary purpose was to extend the construct validity evidence associated with PNSE by linking scores from this instrument with exercise motives and behavioural intentions drawn from a nomological network (Cronbach & Meehl, 1955) implied within the SDT literature (Deci & Ryan, 2002; Vallerand, 2001). Intentions were included in this study for two reasons. First, intentions are considered a proximal determinant of planned behaviour and have been linked with subsequent behaviour in a number of contexts including exercise (see Ajzen, 2005). Second, intentionality is considered a hallmark of motivated behaviour (Ryan, 1995) and poses less measurement problems than indexing actual exercise behaviour (Connor & Sparkes, 2005). Our hypotheses were developed from Deci and Ryan's (1985; 2002) theorizing and previous studies examining issues of psychological need satisfaction in exercise (Edmunds et al., 2006; Vlachopoulos & Michailidou, 2006; Wilson et al., 2003). It was hypothesized that (a) greater satisfaction of psychological needs would be more positively associated with autonomous than controlling forms of exercise motivation and stronger intentions to continue exercising in the future, (2) exercise motivation scores would display a graded pattern of relationships such that proximal motives on SDT's continuum would be more positively associated than distal motives, and (c) autonomous exercise motives would be more positively associated with behavioural intentions to continue exercising than controlled motives.

METHOD

Participants

A total of 176 students and staff drawn from teams enrolled in a university-based physical activity event participated in this study. Participants received no academic credit or remuneration for their involvement. The sample consisted of 84 males (M_{age} = 22.73; SD = 3.51) and 91 females (M_{age} = 22.23; SD = 3.27). One participant did not provide their gender. Participants in this study reported body mass index (BMI) values approximating the healthy range for this age cohort (M_{BMI} males = 23.95; SD = 4.66; M_{BMI} females = 22.12; SD = 2.88) and varied exercise behaviour across the past 7 days ($M_{GLTEQ-METS}$ Males = 40.61; SD = 34.58; $M_{GLTEQ-METS}$ Females = 53.27; SD = 61.74) based on their responses to the Godin Leisure Time Exercise Questionnaire (Godin & Shepherd, 1985). Considering Rodgers and Gauvin's (1998) classification scheme, 51.7% of this sample represents "regular exercisers" given their participation in three or more strenuous exercise sessions/week and 68.2% of the sample reported engaging in exercise on three or more days/week over the past six months.

Measures

Psychological Need Satisfaction in Exercise Scale (PNSE)

Participants completed the 18-item PNSE (Wilson et al., 2006) as an index of their perceived competence, autonomy, and relatedness experienced in exercise contexts. A stem statement anchored each item in terms of how participants usually felt while exercising (i.e., "The following statements represent different feelings people have when they exercise. Please answer the following questions by considering how you typically feel while you are exercising."). Participants responded to each PNSE item (see Table 1) on a scale anchored by 1 (False) and 6 (True). Wilson et al. (2006) supported the structural and convergent validity of PNSE scores and reported internal consistency reliability values exceeding 0.90 across PNSE subscale scores.

Table 1. Standardized loadings and distributional characteristics of PNSE items used in the measurement model analysis

PNSE Latent Factors Item abbreviations	M	SD	Skew.	Kurt.	FL	EV
PNSE – Perceived Competence						
able complete challenging exercises	5.05	0.90	-0.95	1.44	.61	.50
confident I can do challenging exercises	4.59	1.13	-0.65	0.37	.77	.51
confident in exercise ability	4.85	1.08	-1.00	1.01	.85	.33
capable of completing exercises	4.91	1.09	-1.22	1.95	.88	.28
capable of doing challenging exercises	4.70	1.16	-0.90	0.46	.84	.40
feel good about the way I exercise	4.85	1.10	-0.90	0.79	.83	.37
PNSE – Perceived Autonomy						
free to exercise in own way	4.97	1.20	-1.10	0.75	.79	.53
free to make own exercise decisions	4.94	1.15	-1.04	0.98	.87	.31
feel like I am in charge of exercise program	4.90	1.13	-0.90	0.48	.90	.24
I have a say in choosing exercises I do	4.96	1.15	-1.27	1.59	.86	.35
feel free to choose exercise I participate in	4.99	1.11	-1.03	0.83	.87	.31
I decide what exercises I do	5.01	1.14	-1.19	1.29	.88	.30
PNSE – Perceived Relatedness						
feel attached to exercise companions	4.41	1.26	-0.88	0.75	.73	.74
share common bond with important others	4.40	1.27	-0.63	-0.03	.85	.45
feel sense of camaraderie	4.34	1.37	-0.57	-0.27	.78	.74
close to exercise companions	4.41	1.21	-0.62	0.27	.78	.58
feel connected with those I interact with	4.49	1.24	-0.63	-0.02	.85	.42
get along well with other exercisers	4.54	1.26	-0.79	0.51	.84	.46

Note. PNSE = Psychological Need Satisfaction in Exercise Scale (Wilson et al., 2006). Skew. = Univariate Skewness. Kurt. = Univariate Kurtosis.). FL = Factor Loading; EV = Error Variances. FL and EV values are from the CFA of the PNSE measurement model. All FL's are statistically significant at $p < .01$ (two-tailed significance).

Behavioural Regulation in Exercise Questionnaire (BREQ)

Participants completed the BREQ (Mullan et al., 1997), a 15-item self-report measure assessing the reasons why people exercise consistent with SDT. The BREQ operationalizes exercise motivation along a graded self-determination continuum, and includes subscales assessing external, introjected, identified, and intrinsic regulations. Following the stem, "Why do you exercise?", participants respond to each item (see Table 2) on a 5-point Likert scale anchored at the extremes by 1 (Not true for me) and 5 (Very true or me). Previous research has supported the structural validity of BREQ scores (Mullan et al., 1997), and provided evidence of the BREQ scores ability to distinguish active from inactive groups (Mullan & Markland, 1997).

Table 2. Standardized loadings and distributional characteristics of BREQ items used in the measurement model analysis

Instrument Variables Item Abbreviations	M	SD	Skew.	Kurt.	FL	EV
BREQ - External Regulation						
I feel pressured to exercise by friends/family	1.34	1.27	0.49	-0.89	.67	.89
I exercise because others say I should	1.03	1.17	0.92	-0.06	.74	.61
I exercise because others would not be pleased	0.85	1.16	1.22	0.52	.80	.49
I exercise because others say I should	0.91	1.19	1.16	0.26	.84	.41
BREQ - Introjected Regulation						
I feel ashamed when I miss an exercise session	1.63	1.28	0.29	-1.00	.82	.53
I feel guilty when I don't exercise	2.05	1.33	-0.06	-1.11	.80	.62
I feel like a failure when I don't exercise	1.77	1.40	0.20	-1.21	.74	.86
BREQ - Identified Regulation						
I get restless if don't exercise regularly	2.78	1.20	-0.83	-0.19	.67	.78
I think it's important to exercise regularly	3.22	0.94	-1.31	1.67	.88	.20
It's important to me to exercise regularly	3.18	0.99	-1.23	1.09	.88	.22
I value the benefits of exercise	3.34	0.91	-1.66	3.22	.76	.35
BREQ - Intrinsic Regulation						
I find exercise is a pleasurable activity	3.16	0.96	-1.38	1.95	.91	.17
I get pleasure/satisfaction from exercising	3.24	0.93	-1.40	2.00	.87	.22
I exercise because it is fun	3.15	1.02	-1.35	1.51	.80	.37
I enjoy my exercise sessions	3.08	0.98	-1.10	0.93	.86	.25

Note. BREQ = Behavioural Regulation in Exercise Questionnaire (Mullan & Markland, 1997). *FL* = Factor Loading; *EV* = Error Variances. *FL* and *EV* values are from the CFA of the *BREQ* measurement model. All *FL*'s are statistically significant at $p < .01$ (two-tailed significance).

Behavioural Intentions (BI)

Participants completed three items based on Courneya and McAuley's (1993) recommendations to capture intentions to continue exercising over the next 4 months. Following the stem, "These questions concern your exercise plans for the next 4 months', participants responded to each item on a 7-point Likert scale anchored at the extremes by 1 (Strongly Disagree) and 7 (Strongly Agree). Each item was chosen to reflect general intentions ('I intend to exercise regularly during the next 4 months', 'I intend to participate in physical exercise as much as I can every week during the next 4 months') or specific intentions ('I intend to exercise at least 3 times per week over the next 4 months'). Courneya, Nigg, and Estabrooks (1998) supported the criterion validity of scores from these items in terms of their predictive relationship with exercise behaviour.

Procedures and Analyses

Data were collected in small groups (n < 25 in all instances) after participants had been informed about the nature of the investigation and provided the opportunity to ask questions. All participants provided written informed consent prior to participation. Standard instructions were given to each group by the principal investigator to reduce the potential for between groups effects associated with test administration. Subscale scores were created for the PNSE and BREQ subscales, as well as BI, by averaging the relevant items per latent factor (Morris, 1979).

Data analysis proceeded in sequential stages. First, the data were screened for aberrant responses and examined for conformity with statistical assumptions. Second, two confirmatory factor analyses (CFA) using AMOS 6.0 were examined to test the structural validity of PNSE and BREQ responses. Third, descriptive statistics, internal consistency reliability estimates (Coefficient α; Cronbach, 1951), and bivariate correlations were calculated. Fourth, a full measurement model was examined using CFA prior to estimating a structural model that posited behavioural intentions as a function of the degree of relative autonomous exercise motivation which in turn was underpinned by perceived psychological need satisfaction. Conventional standards were specified in all measurement and structural model analyses including correlating latent factors, loading manifest items exclusively on target latent factors, constraining uniqueness values to zero, and fixing a single item loading to unity to define the scale of each factor. A selection of fit indices recommended for use with structural equation modeling (SEM) in small samples were employed to evaluate model fit in both the measurement and structural model analyses (i.e., χ^2, Comparative Fit Index [CFI], Incremental Fit Index [IFI], Root Mean Square Error of Approximation [RMSEA]; West, Finch, & Curran, 1995). While threshold values indicative of acceptable model fit in applications of SEM remain contentious (Hu & Bentler, 1999; Marsh, Hau, & Wen, 2004), CFI and IFI values exceeding 0.90 and 0.95 are considered indicative of acceptable and excellent model fit (Hu & Bentler, 1999). RMSEA values less than 0.05 are desirable whereas values exceeding 0.10 are rarely acceptable (Browne & Cudeck, 1993).

RESULTS

Preliminary Analyses

Only 1.14% missing data was evident across PNSE, BREQ, and BI data with no systematic pattern of non-response evident therefore sample means were imputed (Hawthorne & Elliot, 2005). No extreme responses (> 3 SD's away from the mean per variable/construct) were evident. Item level descriptive statistics indicated some departure from univariate normality in PNSE (see Table 1) and BREQ (see Table 2) scores and notable multivariate kurtosis was evident (Mardia's Coefficient's ranged from 72.67 to 215.40). While alternative estimation procedures exist for data that violate normality assumptions, they require large sample sizes to produce stable parameter estimates and prevent distortion of global model fit estimates (Hu & Bentler, 1999). Maximum likelihood (ML) estimation procedures were employed based West et al.'s (1995) recommendations.

Measurement Model Analysis

Examination of the fit indices (see Table 3) partially supports the tenability of the PNSE and BREQ measurement models. Minimal evidence of over- or under-estimation of fitted correlations in either the PNSE (92.81% $z < |1.0|$; 0% $z > |2.0|$) or BREQ (98.10% $z < |2.0|$; 0% $z > |3.0|$) measurement models were noted in the distribution of standardized residuals. A pattern of moderate-to-strong (all p's < 0.05) standardized parameter estimates were observed across target latent factors scores for each manifest PNSE (Mean $\lambda = 0.82$; $SD = 0.07$) and BREQ (Mean $\lambda = 0.80$; $SD = 0.07$) item. Phi-coefficients from both CFA's indicated a pattern of weak-to-strong relationships between PNSE factors ($\phi_{competence.autonomy} = 0.88$; $\phi_{competence.relatedness} = 0.69$; $\phi_{autonomy.relatedness} = 0.59$; all p's < 0.05) and BREQ factors ($\phi_{external.introjected} = 0.62$; $\phi_{external.identified} = -0.09$; $\phi_{external.intrinsic} = -0.16$; $\phi_{introjected.identified} = 0.41$; $\phi_{introjected.intrinsic} = 0.28$; $\phi_{identified.intrinsic} = 0.88$). Collectively, these results imply that the PNSE and BREQ measurement models appear partially tenable in this sample.

Table 3. Global model fit indices for the measurement and structural models comprised of PNSE, BREQ, and behavioural intentions scores

Models	χ^2	df	p	CFI	IFI	RMSEA (90% CI)
Measurement Models						
Psychological Need Satisfaction in Exercise Scale	334.36	132	< 0.01	0.92	0.92	0.10 (0.08-0.11)
Behavioural Regulation in Exercise Questionnaire	171.79	84	< 0.01	0.94	0.94	0.08 (0.06-0.10)
Full Measurement Model	514.65	242	< 0.01	0.92	0.92	0.08 (0.07-0.09)
Structural Model	399.47	183	< 0.01	0.92	0.92	0.08 (0.07-0.10)

Note. χ^2 = chi-square statistic. df = degrees of freedom. p = probability value. *CFI* = Comparative Fit Index. *IFI* = Incremental Fit Index. *RMSEA* = Root Mean Square Error of Approximation. 90% *CI* = Ninety-percent confidence interval around RMSEA point estimate.

Table 4. Descriptive statistics, internal consistency reliability estimates, and bivariate correlations

Latent Variables	M	SD	Skew.	Kurt	α	1	2	3	4	5	6	7	8
1.PNSE-Perceived Competence	4.82	0.90	-0.82	1.28	0.91	-							
2.PNSE-Perceived Autonomy	4.97	1.00	-0.96	1.19	0.95	.82	-						
3.PNSE-Perceived Relatedness	4.44	1.04	-0.60	0.86	0.92	.65	.58	-					
4.BREQ-External Regulation	1.03	0.99	0.85	0.08	0.85	-.22	-.30	-.06	-				
5.BREQ-Introjected Regulation	1.82	1.15	0.01	-0.91	0.83	.12	.06	.19	.51	-			
6.BREQ-Identified Regulation	3.13	0.85	-1.20	1.72	0.86	.63	.64	.47	-.09	.36	-		
7.BREQ-Intrinsic Regulation	3.16	0.87	-1.47	2.48	0.92	.67	.67	.53	-.15	.23	.79	-	
8.Behavioural Intentions	5.76	1.29	-1.00	0.64	0.89	.49	.43	.32	-.14	.22	.55	.44	-

Note: PNSE = Psychological Need Satisfaction in Exercise scale (Wilson et al., 2006). BREQ = Behavioural Regulation in Exercise Questionnaire (Mullan et al., 1997). M = Univariate Mean. SD = Standard Deviation. *Skew.* = Univariate Skewness. *Kurt.* = Univariate Kurtosis. α = Internal consistency reliability estimates (Cronbach's α; 1951). Bivariate correlations (r) are placed in the lower diagonal of the matrix. Sample size is consistent across each element in the lower triangle of the matrix. All r's are based on pairwise comparison across the elements in the matrix. Each $r \geq |.15|$ is significant at $p < .05$ (two-tailed significance).

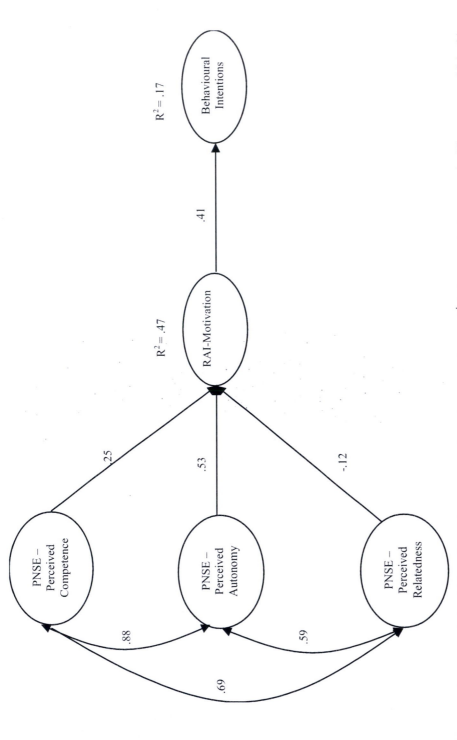

Note: Ellipses represent latent variables used in the SEM analyses. Solid lines indicate ϕ and γ coefficients are significant at $p < .05$ in this sample. $R^2 =$ percentage of variance accounted for in each endogenous latent variable in the SEM analyses.

Figure 1. SEM predicting behavioural intentions from relative autonomous motivation and perceptions of psychological need satisfaction.

Descriptive Statistics, Reliability Estimates, and Bivariate Correlations

Internal consistency reliability estimates ranged from 0.81 to 0.93 across PNSE, BREQ, and BI scores (see Table 4). Participants endorsed greater fulfillment of autonomy followed by competence then relatedness needs in exercise although the magnitude is less pronounced than previously reported (Wilson et al., 2006). Participants reported more autonomous than controlled reasons motivating exercise participation based on the greater endorsement of identified and intrinsic regulations compared with external and introjected regulations, and indicated strong intentions to continue exercising over the next 4 months. An inspection of the bivariate correlations (see Table 4) reveals several interesting patterns of relationships. First, positive relationships were evident between PNSE subscale scores. Second, a quasi-simplex pattern of correlations was evident between BREQ subscale scores whereby regulations adjacent to one another on the SDT continuum are more positively associated with one another than distal regulations. Finally, it appears that greater PNSE scores exhibit more positive correlations with identified and intrinsic regulations than external and introjected regulations.

Structural Equation Modeling Analysis Predicting Exercise Intentions

Consistent with the recommendations of Anderson and Gerbing (1988), a full measurement model was examined prior to evaluating a structural model depicted in Figure 1 drawn from Vallerand's (2001) arguments and theorizing forwarded by Deci and Ryan (2002) in the context of SDT. The full measurement model contained 3 exogenous latent factors (PNSE-Perceived Competence, PNSE-Perceived Autonomy, PNSE-Perceived Relatedness) defined by 6 manifest items/factor, and 2 endogenous latent constructs representing relative autonomous exercise motives (RAI-Motivation) and BI. The latent RAI-Motivation construct was created based on Niemic et al.'s (2005) recommendations. In brief, 3 manifest items were created by computing the average of transformed BREQ item-level responses to define a latent RAI-Motivation factor. The transformation involved weighting the response to each manifest BREQ using the following formula to create transformed items that reflect the degree of relative autonomy underpinning behavioural regulation: (a) External Regulation × -2; (b) Introjected Regulation × -1; (c) Identified Regulation × 1; and (d) Intrinsic Regulation × 2. One transformed item was then selected from each BREQ subscale and averaged to form one of three manifest indicators defining a latent RAI-Motivation construct.

Inspection of the global model fit indices suggested that the full measurement model specified in this analysis differed significantly from the reference independence model (see Table 3). Nevertheless, the pattern of fit indices imply that the full measurement model is tenable and an inspection of the distribution of standardized residuals (99.28% $z < |2.0|$; 0% $z > |3.0|$) suggested little evidence of over- or under-estimation of fitted correlations. A pattern of moderate-to-strong positive loadings were observed for each manifest items on their target latent factors (Mean $\lambda = 0.83$; SD $= 0.06$; all p's < 0.05).

A structural model articulating the relationships between perceived psychological need satisfaction, exercise motivation, and behavioural intentions was specified and tested using SEM procedures advocated for the testing of theory-based models. The model was drawn from Vallerand's (2001) contentions regarding the nature of motivational processes and Deci and Ryan's (2002) development of SDT whereby behavioural intentions were conceptualized as a function of relative autonomous motivation for exercise, which in turn, was underpinned by the satisfaction of competence, autonomy, and relatedness needs. Examination of the structure coefficients (see Figure 1) revealed several noteworthy patterns in the data. First, fulfillment of autonomy needs makes the strongest contribution to predicting exercise motivation followed by perceived competencies while perceived relatedness was negatively associated with endorsement of relative autonomous exercise motivation. Second, greater autonomous motivation for exercise was positively associated with increased intentions to continue exercising over the next 4 months. Finally, the amount of variance accounted for in each endogenous construct corresponds with moderate-to-large effect sizes based on Cohen's (1992) guidelines.

CONCLUSION

The purpose of this study was to examine the contributions of perceived psychological need satisfaction to motivational processes linked with exercise participation. Based on the measurement model analyses, it seems apparent that the PNSE and BREQ display many laudable psychometric characteristics that render both instruments useful for investigating SDT-based arguments in exercise. Perhaps of greater interest in this study is the SEM results that imply the tendency to hold stronger exercise intentions is greater when exercise is autonomously motivated, which in turn, appears to be a function of satisfying psychological needs as suggested within SDT (Deci & Ryan, 2002). Overall, this investigation supports Deci and Ryan's (2002) contention that satisfaction of competence, autonomy, and relatedness needs represent "nutriments" (p.7) essential to motivation and extend their arguments to exercise settings where understanding the processes shaping behaviour has important health implications (Bouchard et al., 2007).

Psychometric Properties of PNSE and BREQ Scores

The measurement model analyses partially supported the structural validity of PNSE and BREQ scores, as well as, the internal consistency reliability of PNSE and BREQ subscale scores. Furthermore, the direction of the inter-factor correlations observed in the CFA's of PNSE and BREQ scores is consistent with SDT and our hypotheses. Notwithstanding this observation, the 95% confidence intervals for the ϕ coefficients between PNSE-Perceived Competence and PNSE-Perceived Autonomy scores and the BREQ-Identified and BREQ-Intrinsic Regulation scores encompassed unity. While this is inconsistent with previous studies (Mullan et al., 1997; Wilson et al., 2006), it highlights the merit of further construct validation research with both instruments. Messick (1995) suggests that construct validation is an ongoing process requiring the constellation of evidence from multiple sources to inform test score interpretation. One avenue to consider in future research concerns the degree of content relevance and representation inherent in the PNSE and BREQ items to determine the unique portion of the content domain captured by each item (Dunn, Bouffard, & Rogers, 1999).

Importance of Motivational Processes

While the results of the SEM analyses support our hypotheses and suggest that autonomous motives are associated with stronger exercise intentions, a substantial portion of the variance in behavioural intentions was left unaccounted for in the structural model. It is possible that a number of other factors influence behavioural intentions that extend beyond the scope of SDT. For example, evidence supporting social ecological approaches for understanding exercise behaviour have been forthcoming (Bauman et al., 2002) and warrant consideration alongside SDT-based claims. Nevertheless, it also seems plausible that the amalgamation of weighted BREQ items into separate manifest indicators for use in the SEM-analyses failed to fully capture subtle variations in extrinsic and intrinsic motivation evident in exercise contexts and impacting behavioural intentions. Koester and Losier (2002) proposed that the use of a single latent construct to represent motivation offers merely global information about reasons for participation. Exemplifying this point, Wilson and colleagues (Wilson & Rodgers, 2002; Wilson et al., 2004) supported the importance of distinguishing between SDT-based motives for understanding the influence of autonomous and controlled motives in exercise contexts on continuance intentions. Nonetheless, the results of this investigation make it apparent that the autonomous (versus controlled) nature of exercise motivation seems crucial for understanding intentional activity, and future studies may wish to counterbalance their desire to use data analytical techniques such as SEM with the potential for losing important information regarding exercise motivation.

The observation that perceived competence and autonomy predict greater reliance on autonomous exercise motivation is consistent with arguments concerning the function of psychological needs during internalization (Deci & Ryan, 2002; Vallerand, 2001). The finding that perceived relatedness was negatively associated with autonomous exercise motivation when considered jointly with other SDT-based needs is less straightforward to reconcile with previous research (Vlachopoulos & Michailidou, 2006). One possible interpretation concerns the degree of statistical overlap inherent in the measurement of latent psychological need satisfaction constructs in the present sample that resulted in net suppression effects in the SEM (Tabachnik & Fidell, 2007). Another plausible interpretation concerns the role of perceived relatedness in exercisers who have internalized their reasons for exercise participation such that behaviour is self-determined and thereby underpinned by authentic perceptions of competence and a sense of volitional agency (Deci & Ryan, 2002). Future studies would do well to address the role of perceived relatedness, in conjunction with other psychological needs outlined by SDT, in those initiating and terminating exercise to determine the salience of social connections to others on motivational processes. Such endeavors will need to be mindful of specifying structural models that represent psychological need satisfaction in global terms (Hagger et al., 2006) versus modeling SDT-based psychological needs individually as exemplified in the present study to prevent the loss of information pertinent to understanding the role played by psychological needs in the nuances of exercise motivation.

Limitations and Future Directions

While the results of this investigation have theoretical and practical merit, a number of limitations require acknowledgement alongside future research directions that may advance our understanding of psychological need satisfaction in exercise contexts. First, this study utilized non-probability based sampling procedures that offer limited external validity. Future research would do well to replicate our study in more diverse populations where exercise motivation is an important issue (e.g., older adults, children) using sampling methods that afford greater confidence in generalizability. Second, despite the tenability of Vallerand's (2001) arguments concerning the temporal sequencing implied in the SEM analyses, the non-experimental nature of the design restricts the causal interpretations that can be made from this study. Future studies could investigate covariation over time between psychological need satisfaction and exercise motivation to provide a more stringent test of Vallerand's contentions. Longitudinal designs would also provide insight into the rate and direction of change inherent in SDT-based psychological needs within exercise settings. Finally, this study focused exclusively on behavioural intentions as a criterion of interest within exercise contexts. Ryan and Deci (2001) argue that psychological needs exert direct and universal effects on well-being (Ryan & Deci, 2001). Future research may wish to examine this assertion to extend the validity evidence of the PNSE and determine the range of well-being markers influenced by the satisfaction of competence, autonomy, and relatedness needs through exercise.

In summary, the purpose of this study was to examine the relationship between perceived psychological need fulfillment in exercise contexts with motives for exercise and behavioural intentions. The results partially supported Vallerand's (2001) assertions regarding the sequence of motivational processes stemming from the satisfaction of SDT-based psychological needs and corroborate Deci and Ryan's (2002) contention that competence, autonomy, and relatedness represent key foundations for the development of more autonomous motives and adaptive consequences in the context of exercise. Furthermore, the results of the measurement model analyses provide mixed support for the validity of PNSE and BREQ scores and suggest continued investigation into the merit of both instruments in exercise contexts would be useful. Overall, the results of this investigation do nothing to undermine Ryan's (1995) assertion that the critical motivational factor responsible for understanding adaptive consequences, such as continuance intentions in exercise settings, concerns the distinction between controlled and autonomous functioning as opposed to the intrinsic or extrinsic nature of the motivation itself. Taken together with previous exercise-based studies (Edmunds et al., 2006; Wilson et al., 2003; Wilson et al., 2006), it seems that SDT may be a useful framework to advance our understanding of motivational issues in exercise contexts and future investigations adopting this theoretical orientation appear worthwhile.

AUTHORS' NOTE

This study was supported by a doctoral fellowship from the Killam Foundation awarded to the first author. The first and second authors were supported by a grant from the Social Sciences and Humanities Research Council of Canada (SSHRC Grant #410-2005-1485) during the preparation of this manuscript. The third author is supported by a SSHRC graduate scholarship.

REFERENCES

Ajzen, I. (2005). *Attitudes, Personality, and Behaviour (2nd Edition)*. Milton Keynes, UK: Open University Press.

Anderson, J. C. & Gerbing, D. W. (1988). Structural equation modeling in practice: A review and recommended two-step approach. *Psychological Bulletin, 103*, 411-423.

Bauman, A.E., Sallis, J.F., Dzewaltowski, D.A., & Owen, N. (2002). Towards a better understanding of the influences on physical activity: The role of determinants, correlates, causal variables, mediators, moderators, confounders. *American Journal of Preventive Medicine, 23*, 5-14.

Baumeister, R. F., & Leary, M. R. (1995). The need to belong: Desire for interpersonal attachments as a fundamental human motivation. *Psychological Bulletin, 117*, 497-529.

Biddle, S. J. H., Fox, K. R., & Boutcher, S. (2000). *Physical Activity and Psychological Well-Being*. London, UK: Routlegde.

Bouchard, C., Blair, S. N., & Haskell, W. L. (2007). *Physical Activity and Health*. Champaign, IL: Human Kinetics.

Browne, M.W., & Cudeck, R. (1993). Alternative ways of assessing model fit. In K.A. Bollen & J.S. Long (Eds.), *Testing Structural Equation Models* (pp. 136-162). Newburg Park, CA: Sage.

Cameron, C., Craig, C. L., & Paolin, S. (2005). *Local opportunities for physical activity and sport: Trends from 1999-2004*. Ottawa. ON: Canadian Fitness & Lifestyle Research Institute.

Craig, C. L., Cameron, R., Russell, S. J., & Beaulieu, A. (2001). *Increasing physical activity: Building a supportive recreation and sport system*. Ottawa. ON: Canadian Fitness & Lifestyle Research Institute.

Conner, M. & Sparks, P. (2005). Theory of planned behaviour and health behaviour. In M. Conner & P. Norman (Eds.), *Predicting Health Behaviour (2nd Edition* pp.170-222). Berkshire, UK: Open University Press.

Courneya, K. S. & McAuley, E. (1993). Predicting physical activity from intention: Conceptual and methodological issues. *Journal of Sport & Exercise Psychology, 5*, 50-62.

Courneya, K. S., Nigg, C., & Estabrooks, P. (1998). Relationships among the theory of planned behaviour, stages of change and exercise behaviour in older persons over a three year period. *Psychology & Health, 13*, 355-367.

Cronbach, L. J. (1951). Coefficient alpha and the internal structure of tests. *Psychometrika, 16*, 297-234.

Cronbach, L. J. & Meehl, P. E. (1955). Construct validity in psychological tests. *Psychological Bulletin, 52,* 281-302.

Cohen, J. (1992). A power primer. *Psychological Bulletin, 112,* 1155-1159.

deCharms, R. (1968). *Personal Causation: The Internal Affective Determinants of Behavior.* New York, NY: Academic Press.

Deci, E. L., & Ryan, R. M. (1985). *Intrinsic Motivation and Self-Determination in Human Behavior.* New York: Plenum Press.

Deci, E. L., & Ryan, R. M. (2002). *Handbook of Self-Determination Research.* Rochester, NY: University of Rochester Press.

Deci, E.L., & Vansteenkiste, M. (2004). Self-determination theory and basic need satisfaction: Understanding human development in positive psychology. *Ricerche di Psicologia, 27,* 17-34.

Dunn, J. G. H., Bouffard, M., & Rogers, W. T. (1999). Assessing item content relevance in sport psychology scale-construction research: Issues and recommendations. *Measurement in Physical Education & Exercise Science, 3,* 15-36.

Godin, G. & Shepherd, R. J. (1985). A simple method to assess exercise behaviour in the community. *Canadian Journal of Applied Sport Sciences, 10,* 141-146.

Edmunds, J., Ntoumanis, N., & Duda, J. L. (2006). Examining exercise dependence symptomology from a self-determination perspective. *Journal of Health Psychology, 6,* 887-903.

Frederick, C. M. & Ryan, R. M. (1993). Differences in motivation for sport and exercise and their relations with participation and mental health. *Journal of Sport Behavior, 16,* 124-146.

Hagger, M. S. & Chatzisarantis, N. (2006). From psychological need satisfaction to intentional behavior: Testing a motivational sequence in two behavioral contexts. *Personality and Social Psychology Bulletin, 32,* 131-138.

Hawthorne, G. & Elliot, P. (2005). Imputing cross-sectional missing data: Comparison of common techniques. *Australian & New Zealand Journal of Psychiatry, 39,* 583-590.

Hu, L. & Bentler, P. M. (1999). Cut-off criteria for fit indexes in covariance structure analysis: Conventional criteria versus new alternatives. *Structural Equation M*odeling, *6,* 1-55.

Koestner, R. & Losier, G. F. (2002). Distinguishing three ways of being highly motivated: A closer look at introjection, identification, and intrinsic motivation. In E. L. Deci & R. M. Ryan (Eds.), *Handbook of Self-Determination Research* (pp. 101-123). Rochester, NY: University of Rochester Press.

Marsh, H.W., Hau, K.T., & Wen, Z. (2004). In search of golden rules: Comment on hypothesis testing approaches to setting cutoff values for fit indexes and dangers in overgeneralizing Hu and Bentler's (1999) findings. *Structural Equation Modeling: A Multidisciplinary Journal, 11,* 320-341.

Messick, S. (1995). Validity of psychological assessment: Validation of inferences from persons' responses and performances as scientific inquiry into score meaning. *American Psychologist, 50,* 741-749.

Morris, J.D. (1979). A comparison of regression prediction accuracy on several types of factor scores. *American Educational Research Journal, 16,* 17-24

Mullan, E., & Markland, D. (1997). Variations in self-determination across the stages of change for exercise in adults. *Motivation & Emotion, 21,* 349-362.

Mullan, E., Markland, D., & Ingledew, D. K. (1997). A graded conceptualization of self-determination in the regulation of exercise behaviour: Development of a measure using confirmatory factor analysis procedures. *Personality & Individual Differences*, *23*, 745-752.

Niemiec, C. P., Lynch, M. F., Vansteenkiste, M., Bernstein, J., Deci, E. L., & Ryan, R. M. (2005). The antecedents and consequences of autonomous self-regulation for college: A self-determination perspective on socialization. *Journal of Adolescence*, *29*, 761-775.

Roberts, G. C. (2001). *Advances in Motivation in Sport and Exercise*. Champaign, IL: Human Kinetics.

Rodgers, W.R., & Gauvin, L. (1998). Heterogeneity of self-efficacy and incentives for physical activity in highly active and moderately active exercisers. *Journal of Applied Social Psychology*, *28*, 1016-1029

Ryan, R. M. (1995). Psychological needs and the facilitation of integrative processes. *Journal of Personality*, *63*, 397-428.

Ryan, R. M., & Deci, E. L. (2001). On happiness and human potentials: A review of research on hedonic and eudaimonic well-being. In S. Fiske (Ed.), *Annual Review of Psychology* (Vol. *52*; pp. 141-166). Palo Alto, CA: Annual Reviews.

Schwartz, B. (2000). The tyranny of freedom. *American Psychologist*, *55*, 79-88.

Sheldon, K. M. (2002). The self-concordance model of health goal striving: When personal goals correctly represent the person. In E. L. Deci & R. M. Ryan (Eds), *The Handbook of Self-Determination Research* (pp. 38-65). Rochester, NY: Rochester University Press.

Sheldon, K. M., Elliot, A. J., Kim, Y., & Kasser, T. (2001). What is satisfying about satisfying events? Testing 10 candidate psychological needs. *Journal of Personality & Social Psychology, 80,* 325-339.

Sheldon, K. M., Williams, G., & Joiner, T. (2003). *Self-Determination Theory in the Clinic-Motivating Physical and Mental Health*. New Haven, CT: Yale University Press.

Tabachnik, L. S., & Fidell, B. (2007). *Using Multivariate Statistics (5th Edition)*. Toronto, ON: Pearson.

Vallerand, R. J. (2001). A hierarchical model of intrinsic and extrinsic motivation in sport and exercise. In G.C. Roberts (Ed.), *Advances in Motivation in Sport and Exercise* (pp. 263-319). Champaign, IL: Human Kinetics.

Vlachopoulos, S. P., & Michailidou, S. (2006). Development and initial validation of a measure of autonomy, competence, and relatedness in exercise: The Basic psychological needs in exercise scale. *Measurement in Physical Education and Exercise Science, 103,* 179-201.

West, S. G., Finch, J. F., & Curran, P. J. (1995). Structural equation models with nonnormal variables: Problems and remedies. In R. H. Hoyle (Ed.), *Structural Equation Modeling: Concepts, Issues, and Applications* (pp. 56-75). Thousand Oaks, CA: Sage.

White, R. W. (1959). Motivation reconsidered: The concept of competence. *Psychological Review*, *66*, 297-333.

Wilson, P. M., & Rodgers, W. M. (2002). The relationship between exercise motives and physical self-esteem in female exercise participants: An application of Self-Determination Theory. *Journal of Applied Biobehavioral Research*, *7*, 30-43.

Wilson, P. M, Rodgers, W. M, Blanchard, C. M, & Gessell, J. (2003). The relationship between psychological needs, self-determined motivation, exercise attitudes, and physical fitness. *Journal of Applied Social Psychology, 33,* 2373-2392.

Wilson, P. M., Rodgers, W. M., Fraser, S. N. & Murray, T. C. (2004). Relationships between exercise regulations and motivational consequences in university students. *Research Quarterly for Exercise & Sport, 75*, 81-91.

Wilson, P. M., Rogers, W. T., Rodgers, W. M., & Wild, T. C. (2006). The psychological need satisfaction in exercise scale. *Journal of Sport & Exercise Psychology, 28*, 231-251.

In: Motivation of Exercise and Physical Activity
Editor: Liam A. Chiang, pp. 53-66

ISBN: 978-1-60021-596-4
© 2007 Nova Science Publishers, Inc.

Chapter 4

PSYCHOLOGY OF MOTIVATIONAL STRUCTURE OF EARLY ADOLESCENTS' PHYSICAL ACTIVITY BEHAVIOR

Bettina F. Piko, Zsuzsanna F. Pluhar and Noémi Keresztes
University of Szeged, Hungary

ABSTRACT

Mapping the motivational structure of adolescents' physical activity behavior is a key point to the development of long term positive attitudes towards sports activity. Unfortunately, after the adolescent period, the level of physical activity seriously declines. However, as longitudinal studies have pointed out, the continuous and regular engagement in sports activity in childhood may increase the likelihood of exercising later in adulthood. Therefore, the main goal of the present study is to detect the motivational structure of early adolescents in distinct school districts in Szeged, Hungary, using a self-administered questionnaire (N=548). The response rate was 91%. Respondents were 10 to 15 years of age (Mean=12.2 years, S.D.=1.2 years) with 54.7 percent of the sample male and 44.9 percent female. A 5-point scale was used to measure the adolescents' motivational structure which contained 18 items derived from the Sport Motivation Scale (SMS). The scale involved both extrinsic and intrinsic types of motivation. Using factor analysis, a four-factor solution has been detected for early adolescents' sport related motivational structure: a "competition and achievement" motivational factor; a "physical fitness, health and sporting attitude" motivational factor; an "external requirements" motivational factor; and a "hedonistic" motivational factor. Both extrinsic and intrinsic motivations are present in the motivational structure of early adolescents related to physical activity. Some of the adolescents are motivated by competitions and prizes, whereas others are motivated by keeping healthy or increasing the level of physical fitness. Some of them are motivated by meeting the requirements of school or parents. In additon, even in this age group, some students are motivated by self-determination, having fun and enjoying the good companion during joint sports activity. Certain differences by sociodemographics and characteristics of sports activity could also be detected.

Keywords: extrinsic and intrinsic motivation; physical activity behavior; early adolescence

INTRODUCTION

Studying physical activity behavior has been recently put in the focus of scientific interests since regular physical activity is an important tool in health promotion and disease prevention (Mutrie & Blamey, 2004). Developing appropriate attitudes towards physical activity is going on during childhood and early adolescence similar to other health related behaviors (Perkins, Jacobs, Barber, & Eccles, 2004). As longitudinal studies have pointed out, the continuous and regular engagement in sports activity in childhood may increase the likelihood of exercising later in adulthood (Telama & Yang, 2000). Unfortunately, after the adolescent period, the level of physical activity seriously declines, particularly during adulthood which has a number of unbeneficial health effects later (Kimm et al., 2000). There is a need to detect the motivational structure of physical activity behavior to maintain its regularity well after the early developmental years. The knowledge of this motivational structure may contribute to the development of health promotion programs which help people benefit from the many positive health effects of physical activity.

Physical activity behavior, similar to other health related behaviors, is closely connected to the theories of motivation based on social cognitive models. For example, the Theory of Planned Behavior (TPB) states that the decision of an individual's behavior is a reasoned action (Ajzen & Madden, 1986). In the middle of the model, there is an intention influenced by many behavioral, normative and controlling factors, for example, other persons' beliefs of a certain behavior or the individual's idea that he or she wants to meet this normative belief. The model also implies the presence or absence of controlling factors which may contribute to the extrinsic or intrinsic nature of a motivation leading to a certain behavior (Hagger, Chatzisarantis, & Biddle, 2002). While behavioral control is crucial in this process, changes in normative pressures may contribute to a less positive attitude towards exercise after the age of 14 years (Godin & Shephard, 1986).

Besides the Theory of Planned Behavior, the Theory of Self-Determination is another frequently applied theoretical framework for motivational studies developed by Deci and Ryan (1985). This model primarily focuses on the psychological needs for self-determination, self-actualization and personal growth. Similar to the Theory of Planned Behavior, it also emphasizes the social context and its effects on intrinsic motivation (Ryan & Deci, 2000). These basic psychological needs, for example, the need for autonomy, self-efficacy or social acceptance, play an important role in developing intrinsic motivations to physical activity or other health related behaviors (Ntoumanis, 2001; Wang & Biddle, 2001). This model also highlights the pleasure function of sports activity, that is, the close relationship between motivations and emotions which may contribute to the maintenance of regular physical activity (Frederick, Morrison, & Manning, 1996).

Among the models explaning motivations to physical activity, the Achievement Goal Theory mainly concentrates on the achievement oriented motivations such as task orientation (when the person defines success based on his/her mastery and developments in achievements) or self-orientation (when the person defines success based on outplaying other persons) (Treasure & Roberts, 1995). These motivations are primarily important for those engaging in sporting competitions (Thomassen & Halvari, 1996). Similar to the previous models, this theory also may be connected to the structure of extrinsic or intrinsic motivations in such that task orientation is related to intrinsic motivations while self-orientation may not be linked to either extrinsic or intrinsic motivations in terms of sports activity (Whitehead, 1995). However, Cervello and Santos-Rosa (2001) have described the self-oriented and negative task oriented motivations as maladaptive factors in relation with sporting motivations. In relation with this model, we should also take into account theoretical models based on the beliefs of one's ability. For example, sports performance is influenced by the person's belief of his/her own ability which may have an impact on the motivational structure. The lack of such beliefs may lead to amotivation through a detrimental effect of lowered self-efficacy (Biddle, Soos, & Chatzisarantis, 1999).

Based on the literature review, most motivational theories imply the simple model of grouping motivations as either *extrinsic* or *intrinsic*. However, Hagger, Chatzisarantis and Biddle (2002) have come to a conclusion that based on the locus of motivations, the motivational structure may be viewed more as a continuum than a dichotomous construct. Their model is called Perceived Locus of Causality (PLOC) which involves four independent scales designed to measure motivations. The degree of autonomy is the determinant of the perceived locus of causality continuum which makes a difference among the motivational scales. At the end of the continuum, the *intrinsic motivation* scale means the choice of physical activity for enjoyment, pleasure and fun, that is, spontaneous activity in general. Next to this, the *identification* as a motivation is characterized by personally held values, such as learning new skills or gaining feelings of satisfaction or pride. The *introjection* as motivation is closer to external (extrinsic) motivations, but is also different from them characterized as participation in physical activity due to such feelings like social pressure (that is, external pressure), guilt or shame. Finally, the other end of the continuum may be characterized by external regulation, such as external reinforcement or gaining rewards and avoiding punishment. All these are pure *extrinsic* motivations. Intrinsic motivations belong to high autonomy and may be called autonomous motivation, whereas external/extrinsic motivations may be called controlling motivations due to their low levels of autonomy.

We must also note that the motivational structure of physical activity behavior undergoes tremendous changes according to age (Campbell et al., 2001). Whereas among adults, health motivations play the most significant role in the engagement in physical activity, among children, the motivational structure is much wider implying both social and psychological factors, extrinsic and intrinsic motivations (Ntoumanis, 2001).

Social factors, similar to other health related behaviors, have a strong influence on a person's attitudes toward sports activity (Sallis et al., 1992). The social learning theory (Bandura, 1986) emphasizes the role of the person's social network, most often the closest social environment, for example, the best friend (Piko, 2001). Physically active peers may be a strong resource of positive motivations which may be increased by the adolescents' need for peer group conformity, particularly among female adolescents (Higgins et al., 2003). Social influences also involve the motivating role of parents, other family members, teachers and coaches, besides peers (Smith, 2003). In addition, social environmental effects also mean a wider social context, that is, the role of sociocultural value system and social norms of society as well as the role of media and a general societal attitude towards physical activity (Hassandra, Goudas, & Chroni, 2003).

By growing age, intrinsic motivations become dominant, particularly among those adults whose engagement in physical activity is not regular (Campbell et al., 2001). Among the younger generations, however, extrinsic motivations are likewise important, such as personal achievement and success or the social acceptance of these (Duda et al., 1992). In the study of Longhurst and Spink (1987), children report dominantly extrinsic and social motivations in relation with their engagement in physical activity. However, the intrinsic motivations are also present even in small children. A person's psychological needs (e.g., higher level of self-efficacy or better psychological well-being), social needs (e.g., popularity among peers, pleasure stemming from the joint activity) and the desired physiological effects (e.g., a better figure, muscular status or higher fitness level) all are present in children's motivational structure (Goudas, Biddle, & Fox, 1994).

Besides age, gender is also an important influence of the motivational structure related to physical activity. A basic finding is that females are less motivated (particularly in terms of extrinsic motivations) and engaged in less physical activity (Wang & Biddle, 2001). In additon, displaying power, trying abilities or achieving success are more important for boys, whereas pleasure or joint activity are more important for girls (Viira & Raudsepp, 2000). Finally, boys are more engaged in organized sport than girls (Pikó, 2000; Vilhjalmsson & Kristjansdottir, 2003).

Beyond sociodemographics, certain personality factors also influence the motivational structure. For example, attitudes towards competitions, achievement orientations, curiosity or risk taking tendencies are important determinants of sports motivations, particularly in terms of certain types of sport (Reiss, Wiltz, & Sherman, 2001). Likewise, individualistic or collectivistic attitudes may also influence achievement orientation, and therefore, the motivational structure (Hayashi, 1996).

Based on the literature review, we must conclude that mapping the motivational structure of adolescents' physical activity behavior seems to be an important research field. This is a key point to the development of long term positive attitudes towards sports activity. Therefore, the main goal of the present study is to detect the motivational structure of early adolescents (aged between 10-15 years).

METHODS

Participants and Procedures

Data were collected from middle school students using randomly selected classes from four schools in different school districts in Szeged, Hungary. The total number of students sampled was 600. Of the questionnaires distributed, 548 were returned and analyzed, yielding a response rate of 92 percent. The age range of the respondents was 10 to 15 years of age (Mean = 12.2 years, S.D. = 1.2 years) and 54.7 percent of the sample was male. We selected this age group, because at this age, children usually report a high level of sports activity, therefore, the engagement in physical activity is an integrated part of their lifestyle.

Data were collected during Fall 2003, using a self-administered questionnaire. Parents were informed of the study with their consent obtained prior to data collection. A standardized procedure of administration was followed. Trained graduate students distributed the questionnaires to students in each class after briefly explaining the study objectives and giving the necessary instructions. Students completed the questionnaires during the class period. The quesionnaires were anonymous and voluntary.

Measures

The self-administered questionnaires contained items on physical activity behavior, its motivational structure as well as some basic sociodemographics (age, gender, parental schooling and SES self-assessment); and some other items on sport, such as the levels of sports activity.

Regarding physical activity behavior, the following question was asked: "How many times in the last three months have you exercised (for at least a half hour)?" Response categories were not even in school = 0, no extra sport just in school = 1, occasionally = 2, once or twice a month = 3, once or twice a week = 4, and three or more times a week = 5 (Luszczynska et al., 2004; Piko & Keresztes, 2006). In further analyses, these responses were recoded using three categories indicating a non-active group (no extra physical activity beyond school), a less active group (just occasionally) and a regularly active group (minimum two or three times a month).

Mapping the adolescents' motivational structure, a 5-point scale was used which contained 18 items derived from the Sport Motivation Scale (SMS) developed by Pelletier and his coworkers (Pelletier et al., 1995). The scale involved both extrinsic and intrinsic types of motivation. The motivations were applied based on an adaptation to the age of the children, for example, the role of parents and teachers or the children's future sport related plans were implied. Factor analysis was used to detect the motivational structure based on the items of the scale. The summary scores of the motivational factors were then analyzed by gender, school year, SES self-assessment (Piko & Fitzpatrick, 2001), sporting behavior, the type of sport, and the levels of sports activity.

Statistical Analyses

Factor analysis with varimax rotation was conducted to detect the motivational structure. Eigenvalues above 1 were applied as the point to stop extracting factors. Variance explained was also calculated. In the final factor structure, factor loadings greater than 0.3 were included (Kaiser's criterion). The significant motivational variables were then summarized and the reliability for each scale was calculated. In the further analyses, the mean scores of the scales were included by using ANOVA and t-tests.

Table 1. Final factor structure for the sport related motivations among early adolescents

Factors with eigenvalues

Motivations	Factor 1 (4.69)	Factor 2 (3.40)	Factor 3 (1.82)	Factor 4 (1.76)
		Factor loadings		
1. I would like to meet the school's requirement	-	-	0.745	-
2. I would like to meet my parents' requirement	-	-	0.836	-
3. I would like to make my parents happy	-	0.353	0.579	-
4. I would like to be healthier	-	0.631	-	0.304
5. I would like better physical fitness	-	0.724	-	0.314
6. I would like a better figure	-	0.733	-	-
7. I would like heavier muscles	-	0.752	-	-
8. I would like to enjoy that I have the power over my body	-	0.726	-	-
9. I would like to become a good sportsman	0.713	0.431	-	-
10. I would like to become similar to the elite sportsmen	0.774	0.367	-	-
11. I would like to achieve my coach's satisfaction	0.582	0.344	-	-
12. I would like to enjoy competitions and prizes	0.770	-	-	-
13. I would like to enjoy the feeling of being a winner	0.733	-	-	-
14. I would like to be famous	0.815	-	-	-
15. I would like to enjoy the encouragement of fans	0.649	-	-	0.374
16. I would like to get popular among peers	0.791	-	-	-
17. I would like to enjoy the good companion of peers	-	-	-	0.743
18. I would like to have fun	-	-	-	0.804
Cronbach's alpha	0.91	0.87	0.63	0.76
% variance	26.0	18.9	10.1	9.8

Note: Only factort loadings > 0.3 are included (Kaiser's criterion). Cronbach's alpha coefficients display the reliability of the scales.

RESULTS

Factor analysis was conducted to detect the sport related motivational structure of youth. The analysis provided a four-factor solution with good reliability values (Cronbach's alpha). Eigenvalues above 1 were applied as the point to stop extracting factors. Variance explained was 64.8 per cent. Table 1 presents the final factor structure for this solution in which only factor loadings greater than 0.3 were included (Kaiser's criterion).

Factor 1 was labelled "competition and achievement" motivational factor which is closely connected to extrinsic motivations such as being famous and popular, enjoying competitions, prizes, the encouragement of fans, becoming similar to elite sportsmen, achieving the coach's satisfaction, etc. The strongest factor loading is connected to the motivation "becoming famous", that is, ambition is a key element of this motivational factor.

Factor 2 was labelled "physical fitness, health and sporting attitude" motivational factor which includes the various items of motivations, that is, this is a mixed motivational factor including both intrinsic and extrinsic items. Therefore, this factor expresses the variety of different motivations and the interconnections among them. Similar to the first factor, achieving the coach's satisfaction or becoming a good sportsman as motivations are also present here. However, intrinsic motivations also appear such as items related to physical fitness, figure or making the parents happy.

Table 2. Influences between "competition and achievement" motivational factor (scores: 8-40) and sociodemographic and sports variables

Influencing factors	Attributes	Means (S.D.)	Significance
Gender	Boys	26.0 (8.8)	$p < 0.05$, t-test
	Girls	24.4 (8.5)	
SES self-assessment	Lower class	22.0 (12.3)	$p < 0.05$, ANOVA
	Lower-middle class	20.8 (9.2)	
	Middle class	25.0 (8.6)	
	Upper-middle class	26.0 (8.3)	
	Upper class	27.5 (9.6)	
School grade	5th grade	24.2 (8.0)	$p > 0.05$, ANOVA
	6th grade	25.9 (9.2)	
	7th grade	25.8 (9.0)	
	8th grade	25.4 (8.6)	
Type of sport	Individual sport	24.0 (8.7)	$p < 0.001$, t-test
	Team sport	28.6 (7.3)	
Level of sport	International/national	32.2 (6.1)	$p < 0.001$, ANOVA
	County/town	28.2 (7.3)	
	Not competitive	19.9 (7.7)	
	No but will	26.0 (7.0)	
Frequency of sport	Only at school	20.3 (8.8)	$p < 0.001$, ANOVA
	Occasionally	20.0 (7.7)	
	Regularly	27.7 (7.9)	

Factor 3 was labelled "external requirements" motivational factor which includes a desire to meet the requirement of school or parents.

And finally, factor 4 was labelled "hedonistic" motivational factor. This factor dominantly includes social motivations, such as having fun, enjoying the good companion and the encouragement of fans. Besides these motivations, health and physical fitness also appear. This motivational factor expresses intrinsic motivations.

Based on the factor loadings, four motivational scales were developed with satisfactory reliability (Table 1). In further analyses, the mean scores of the scales were applied and analyzed according to various sociodemographics and sports characteristics.

Table 2 displays the relationship between factor 1 and other variables including sociodemographics (such as gender, SES, age) and the characteristics of physical activity (such as the type, frequency and level of sport). The competition and achievement motivational factor seems to be more important for those who are boys ($p<.05$), from upper and upper middle classes ($p<.05$), are engaged in regular and team sports ($p<.001$), and competitions (or at least plan it) ($p<.001$).

Table 3 shows the results related to factor 2. A similar picture of influences appear: the mixed motivation factor seems to be more important for boys, upper class children, and those who are engaged in team sports, regular sports and competitions.

Table 4 presents the results related to the external factor. Unlike the previous two factors, there are no significant differences by gender in the mean scores. The other sociodemographic or sport related variables do not show any differences.

Table 3. Influences between "physical fitness, health and sporting attitude" motivational factor (scores: 9-45) and sociodemographic and sports variables

Influencing variables	Attributes	Means (S.D.)	Significance
Gender	Boys	33.6 (7.8)	$p<0.001$, t-test
	Girls	31.1 (7.1)	
SES self-assessment	Lower class	30.0 (18.2)	$p<0.01$, ANOVA
	Lower-middle class	27.8 (8.5)	
	Middle class	32.5 (7.3)	
	Upper-middle class	32.8 (7.3)	
	Upper class	35.4 (8.6)	
School grade	5th grade	31.4 (7.5)	$p>0.05$, ANOVA
	6th grade	32.8 (8.2)	
	7th grade	33.1 (8.2)	
	8th grade	32.9 (7.6)	
Type of sport	Individual sport	32.2 (7.2)	$p<0.05$, t-test
	Team sport	35.2 (6.3)	
Level of sport	International/national	37.3 (6.2)	$p<0.001$, ANOVA
	County/town	34.9 (6.1)	
	Not competitive	28.7 (7.2)	
	No but will	32.5 (7.6)	
Frequency of sport	Only at school	26.7 (8.5)	$p<0.001$, ANOVA
	Occasionally	29.2 (6.4)	
	Regularly	34.5 (6.7)	

Table 4. Influences between "external requirements" motivational factor (scores: 3-15) and sociodemographic and sports variables

Influencing variables	Attributes	Means (S.D.)	Significance
Gender	Boys	8.3 (3.0)	p>0.05, t-test
	Girls	8.7 (2.8)	
SES self-assessment	Lower class	8.6 (4.9)	p<0.01, ANOVA
	Lower-middle class	7.1 (2.8)	
	Middle class	8.4 (2.7)	
	Upper-middle class	8.6 (3.0)	
	Upper class	9.9 (3.2)	
School grade	5th grade	8.6 (4.9)	p>0.05, ANOVA
	6th grade	7.1 (2.8)	
	7th grade	8.4 (2.7)	
	8th grade	8.6 (3.0)	
Type of sport	Individual sport	8.7 (2.7)	p>0.05, t-test
	Team sport	8.7 (3.0)	
Level of sport	International/national	9.0 (2.9)	p>0.05, ANOVA
	County/town	8.4 (2.7)	
	Not competitive	8.3 (3.0)	
	No but will	8.7 (3.1)	
Frequency of sport	Only at school	8.1 (3.0)	p>0.05, ANOVA
	Occasionally	8.3 (2.6)	
	Regularly	8.7 (3.0)	

Table 5. Influences between "hedonistic" motivational factor (scores: 5-25) and sociodemographic and sports variables

Influencing variables	Attributes	Means (S.D.)	Significance
Gender	Boys	19.0 (4.1)	p>0.05, t-test
	Girls	18.8 (3.8)	
SES self-assessment	Lower class	18.4 (7.9)	p>0.05, ANOVA
	Lower-middle class	17.1 (5.0)	
	Middle class	18.8 (4.1)	
	Upper-middle class	19.2 (3.3)	
	Upper class	19.7 (4.1)	
School grade	5th grade	17.9 (4.0)	p<0.01, ANOVA
	6th grade	18.9 (4.3)	
	7th grade	19.5 (3.9)	
	8th grade	19.5 (4.0)	
Type of sport	Individual sport	18.8 (3.5)	p>0.05, t-test
	Team sport	19.9 (3.4)	
Level of sport	International/national	20.9 (3.2)	p<0.001, ANOVA
	County/town	19.8 (3.5)	
	Not competitive	17.6 (4.1)	
	No but will	18.6 (3.3)	
Frequency of sport	Only at school	16.4 (5.4)	p<0.001, ANOVA
	Occasionally	18.0 (3.7)	
	Regularly	19.6 (3.5)	

Table 5 shows the relationship between the hedonistic motivational factor and other variables of the study. There are differences in the mean scores according to age (school grade): the dominantly intrinsic motivations seem to be more important for older students. Gender or SES do not seem to be determinant.

DISCUSSION

The primary goal of our study has been to detect the motivational structure of early adolescents' physical activity behavior. Previous study reveal that motivations play an important role in determining sport related attitudes on long term (Campbell et al., 2001). The positive attitudes towards sport should be developed during childhood to prevent a serious decline of sports activity later. The motivational structure is strongly influenced by age, gender, the type and level of sports activity. During the years of adolescence, social influences are rather strong. Whereas peer groups appear to be the most determinant for late adolescents, the role of relevant adults (parents, coaches, teachers) is still important for early adolescents (Sallis et al., 1992; Smith, 2003). Age also significantly contributes to the change of the motivational structure; there is an increase of the significance of intrinsic factors which become dominant in adulthood (Campbell et al., 2001; Duda et al., 1992; Ntoumanis, 2001).

Using factor analysis, a four-factor solution has been detected for early adolescents' sport related motivational structure: a "competition and achievement" motivational factor; a "physical fitness, health and sporting attitude" motivational factor; an "external requirements" motivational factor; and a "hedonistic" motivational factor. Whereas the first and the third factors are dominantly based on extrinsic motivations, the second and the fourth factors primarily include intrinsic motivations. However, only the fourth factor involves such motivations like having fun with a peer group which is more determinant during late adolescence (Anderssen & Wold, 1992). The second factor involves both extrinsic and intrinsic motivations in a well-balanced way. Those who prefer this type of motivations are not only competiton and achievement oriented but also interested in the effects of sports activity on health and physical fitness. This type of motivation may be called identification based on the study of Hagger et al. (2002), completed with some important extrinsic items of motivation. The third factor, characterized by external motivations, is typical in this age group but its significance tends to decrease during late adolescence. This factor is close to the motivation called introjection by Hagger et al. (2002), that is, an introjection of external effects such as social pressure from parents and the school.

As the literature suggests, the motivational structures of boys and girls are different (Wang & Biddle, 2001; Viira & Raudsepp, 2000; Pikó 2000; Vilhjalmsson & Kristjansdottir, 2003). Our results suggest that not only the extrinsic but also the intrinsic motivations are more common among boys. One exemption is meeting external requirements which is slightly more common among girls, however, the difference is below the level of significance. Age is another sociodemographic factor influencing the motivational structure. Our findings suggest that hedonistic motivations are getting more common by age parallel with the increasing peer group effect. The mean score of this motivational factor is the lowest among students from 5th grade, whereas it is the highest among those from 7th and 8th grades.

The relationship between physical activity behavior and socioeconomic status is rather complex. A previous study reveal that upper and upper middle class students are engaged in the highest levels of physical activity (Tuinstra et al., 1998). However, our previous results on Hungarian adolescents show a J shaped figure, that is, besides the highest level of physical activity among the upper class students, those from the lowest SES also scored relatively higher on sports activity (Keresztes & Piko, 2006). The relationship between sport related motivations and SES shows similar picture including all types of motivations whether extrinsic or intrinsic. The only exception is the hedonistic motivation.

Characteristics of sports activity such as the type, level and frequency of physical activity also influence the motivational structure. For example, those who are engaged in team sports report higher levels of motivations whether extrinsic or intrinsic as well as they are more competition and achievement oriented. One explanation is that those who take exercise solely are less likely to be involved in competitive sports activity. The relationship between the level of sports activity and the motivational structure supports this idea; those who are engaged in competitions at higher levels are more motivated in regular engagement in physical activity. Another interesting point is that those who are not involved in competitive sports activity at present but intend to get involved in such events report higher levels of motivations. This underlines the role of intention in a person's behavioral decisions ((Ajzen & Madden, 1986). Finally, not surprisingly, there is a close connection between the frequency of sports activity and the levels of motivation; however, this is not a mere cause and effect relationship (which may not be justified in our cross-sectional study) but more a bidirectional connection.

As a summary, we may conclude that both extrinsic and intrinsic motivations are present in the motivational structure of early adolescents related to physical activity. Some of the adolescents are motivated by competitions and prizes, whereas others are motivated by keeping healthy or increasing the level of physical fitness. Some of them are motivated by meeting the requirements of school or parents. In additon, even in this age group, some students are motivated by self-determination, having fun and enjoying the good companion during joint sports activity.

In health promotion programs, we must develop a balance between extrinsic and intrinsic motivations. Physical activity behavior is closely connected to other health related behaviors such as smoking or drug use; adolescents who are regularly engaged in sports activity are also less likely to smoke or use illicit drugs (Pate et al., 1996). This is associated with the internal locus of control, that is, a protective psychological factor against substance use and other unhealthy behaviors. Mapping the motivational structure of health related behaviors has important implications for prevention during adolescence (Casey et al., 1993).

REFERENCES

Ajzen, I., & Madden, T.J. (1986). Prediction of goal-directed behavior: attitudes, intentions and perceived behavioral control. *Journal of Experimental Social Psychology,* 22, 453–474.

Anderssen, N., & Wold, B. (1992). Parental and peer influences on leisure–time physical activity in young adolescents. *Research Quarterly for Exercise and Sport,* 63, 341–348.

Bandura, A. (1986). *Social foundations of thought and action: A social cognitive theory.* Prentice Hall, Englewood Cliffs, N.J.

Biddle, S., Soos, I., & Chatzisarantis, N. (1999). Predicting physical activity intentions using a goal perspectives approach: A study of Hungarian youth. *Scandinavian Journal of Medicine and Science in Sports,* 9, 353-357.

Campbell, P.G., Macauley, D., McCrum, E., & Evans, A. (2001). Age differences in motivating factors for exercise. *Journal of Sport & Exercise Psychology,* 23, 191-199.

Casey, T.A., Kingery, P.M., Bowden, R.G., & Corbett, B.S. (1993). An investigation of the factor structure of the Multidimensional Health Locus of Control scales in a health promotion program. *Educational and Psychological Measurement,* 53, 491-498.

Cervello, E.M., & Santos-Rosa, F.J. (2001). Motivation in sport: An achievement goal perspective in young Spanish recreational athletes. *Perception and Motor Skills,* 92, 527-534.

Deci, E.L., & Ryan, R.M. (1985). *Intrinsic motivation and self-determination in human behavior.* Plenum Press, New York.

Duda, JL., Fox, K.R., Biddle, S.J.H., & Armstrong, N. (1992). Children's achievement goals and beliefs about success in sport. *British Journal of Educational Psychology,* 62, 313-323.

Frederick, C.M., Morrison, C., & Manning, T. (1996). Motivation to participate, exercise affect, and outcome behaviors toward physical activity. *Perception and Motor Skills,* 82, 691-701.

Godin, G., & Shephard, R.J. (1986). Normative beliefs of school children concerning regular exercise. *Journal of School Health,* 54, 443-445.

Goudas, M., Biddle, S., & Fox, K. (1994). Achievement goal orientations and intrinsic motivation in physical fitness testing with children. *Pediatric Exercise Science,* 6, 159-167.

Hagger, M.S., Chatzisarantis, N.L.D. & Biddle, S.J.H. (2002). The influence of autonomous and controlling motives on physical activity intentions within the Theory of Planned Behaviour. *British Journal of Health Psychology,* 7, 283-297.

Hassandra, M., Goudas, M., & Chroni, S. (2003). Examining factors associated with intrinsic motivation in physical education: A qualitative approach. *Psychology of Sport and Exercise,* 4, 211-223.

Hayashi, C.T. (1996). Achievement motivation among Anglo-American and Hawaiian male physical activity participants: Individual differences and social contextual factors. *Journal of Sport and Exercise Psychology,* 18, 194-215.

Higgins, W.J., Gaul, C., Gibbons, S., & Van Gyn, G. (2003). Factors influencing physical activity levels among Canadian youth. *Canadian Journal of Public Health,* 94, 45-51.

Keresztes N., & Pikó B. (2006). Determining sociodemographic factors of youth's physical activity in the Southern Plain Region. *Hungarian Review of Sport Science,* 7, 7-12. (in Hungarian).

Kimm, S.Y.S., Glynn, N.W., Kriska, A.M., Fitzgerald, S.L., Aaron, D.J., Similo, S.L., McMahon, R.P., & Marton, B.A. (2000). Longitudinal changes in physical activity in a biracial cohort during adolescence. *Medicine and Science in Sports and Exercise,* 32, 1445-1454.

Longhurst, K., & Spink, K.S. (1987). Participation motivation of Australian children involved in organized sport. *Canadian Journal of Sport Science,* 12, 24-30.

Luszczynska, A., Gibbons, F.X., Piko, B.F., & Teközel, M. (2004). Self-regulatory cognitions, social comparison, and perceived peers' behaviors as predictors of nutrition and physical activity: A comparison among adolescents in Hungary, Poland, Turkey, and USA. *Psychology and Health, 19*, 577-593.

Mutrie, N., & Blamey, A. (2004). Getting the inactive implications for public health policy. *Journal of the Royal Society for the Promotion of Health, 124*, 16-17.

Ntoumanis, N. (2001). A self-determination approach to the understanding of motivation in physical education. *British Journal of Educational Psychology, 71*, 225-242.

Pate, R.R., Heath, G.W., Dowda, M., & Trost, S.G. (1996). Associations between physical activity and other health behaviors in a representative sample of US adolescents. *American Journal of Public Health, 86*, 1577-1581.

Pelletier, L.G., Fortier, M.S., Vallerand, R.J., Tison, K.M., et al. (1995). Toward a new measure of intrinsic motivation, extrinsic motivation, and amotivation in sports: The Sport Motivation Scale (SMS). *Journal of Sport and Exercise Psychology, 17*, 35-53.

Perkins, D.F., Jacobs, J.E., Barber, B.L., & Eccles, J.S. (2004). Childhood and adolescent sport participation as predictors of participation in sports and fitness activities during young adulthood. *Youth & Society, 35*, 495-520.

Piko, B., & Fitzpatrick, K.M. (2001). Does class matter? SES and psychosocial health among Hungarian adolescents. *Social Science and Medicine, 53*, 817-830.

Piko, B. (2000). Health-related predictors of self-perceived health in a student population: The importance of physical activity. *Journal of Community Health, 25*, 125-137.

Piko, B. (2001). Smoking in adolescence: Do attitudes matter? *Addictive Behaviors, 26*, 201-217.

Piko, B. F., & Keresztes, N. (2006). Physical activity, psychosocial health and life goals among youth. *Journal of Community Health, 31*, 136-145.

Reiss, S., Wiltz, J., & Sherman, M. (2001). Trait motivational correlates of athleticism. *Personality and Individual Differences, 30*, 1139-1145.

Ryan, R.M., & Deci, E.L. (2000). Self-determination theory and the facilitation of intrinsic motivation, social development, and well-being. *American Psychologist, 55*, 68-78.

Sallis, J.F., Hovell, M.F., Hofstetter, C.R., & Barrington, E. (1992). Explanation of vigorous physical activity during two years using social learning variables. *Social Science and Medicine, 34*, 25-32.

Smith, A.L. (2003). Peer relationships in physical activity contexts: A road less traveled in youth sport and exercise psychology research. *Psychology of Sport and Exercise, 4*, 25-39.

Telama, R., & Yang, X., (2000). Decline of physical activity from youth to young adulthood in Finland. *Medicine and Science in Sports and Exercise, 32*, 1617-1622.

Thomassen, T.O., & Halvari, H. (1996). Achievement motivation and involvement in sport competitions. *Perception and Motor Skills, 83*, 1363-1374.

Treasure, D., & Roberts, G.V. (1995). Applications of achievement goal theory to physical education: Implications for enhancing motivation. *Quest, 47*, 475-489.

Tuinstra, J., Groothoff, J.W., van den Heuvel, W.J., & Post, D. (1998). Socio-economic differences in health risk behavior in adolescence: Do they exist? *Social Science & Medicine, 47*, 67-74.

Viira, R., & Raudsepp, L. (2000). Achievement goal orientations, beliefs about sport success and sport emotions as related to moderate to vigorous physical activity of adolescents. *Psychology and Health,* 15, 625-633.

Vilhjalmsson, R., & Kristjansdottir, G. (2003). Gender differences in physical activity in older children and adolescents: The central role of organized sport. *Social Science and Medicine*, 56, 363-374.

Wang, C.K.J., & Biddle, S.J.H. (2001). Young people's motivational profiles in physical activity: A cluster analysis. *Journal of Sport & Exercise Psychology*, 23, 1-22.

Whitehead, J. (1995). Multiple achievement orientations and participation in youth sport: A cultural and developmental perspective. *International Journal of Sport Psychology,* 26, 431-452.

In: Motivation of Exercise and Physical Activity
Editor: Liam A. Chiang, pp. 67-77

ISBN: 978-1-60021-596-4
© 2007 Nova Science Publishers, Inc.

Chapter 5

EDUCATION THROUGH THE PHYSICAL: THE EFFECTIVENESS OF TEACHING LIFE SKILLS PROGRAM IN PHYSICAL EDUCATION

Vassilios Papacharisis[1,], Grigorios Theofanidis[1] and Steven Danish[2]*

[1]Aristotle University of Thessaloniki, Greece
[2]Virginia Commonwealth University, USA

ABSTRACT

The purpose of the present study was to examine the effect of a life skills program taught in the school setting through physical education classes. The participants were 97 students (59 boys, 38 girls), aged from 10 to 12 years ($M = 11,16$, $SD = .64$). Students were evaluated regarding their: (a) performance in sport skills; (b) knowledge about life skills; (c) self – assessment of their ability to use life skills; and (d) their sense of self – efficiency about their sport skills performance before and after implementation of the program. The results of the study support the effectiveness of a program that integrates physical education curriculum and life- skills training. Students who participate in such program can improve their sports skills, while at the same time the inclusion of life skills training into practice may serve as an effective model for learning life – skills.

Keywords: physical education curriculum, life skills development

* Please address correspondence to: Dr. Vassilios Papacharisis, Aristotle University of Thessaloniki, Division of Intercollegiate Athletics, University Gymnasium, 54124 Thessaloniki, Greece. Email: vaspap@phed.auth.gr; +30 2310 992673

INTRODUCTION

It is understood that active children are less likely to be obese and more likely to pursue sporting activity as adults. More recently, educators have become aware that there are non-athletic skills can improve athletic performance. These skills are called *sport psychology skills*. What is less well understood is that these same skills can improve student concentration, commitment and self-esteem in the classroom. When the skills improve performance in non-sport domains, they are called *life* skills.

Life skills can be behavioral (e.g., communicating effectively) or cognitive (making effective decisions); interpersonal (being assertive) or intrapersonal (setting goals) (Danish, Petitpas, & Hale, 1995). The World Health Organization (1999) defines life skills as the abilities for adaptive and positive behavior that enable individuals to deal effectively with the demands and challenges of every day life. These skills can help individuals make informed decisions, communicate effectively, and develop coping and self-management abilities that may help them lead a healthy and productive life. Teaching life skills is essential for the promotion of healthy child and adolescent development, and for preparing young people for their changing social circumstances.

The belief that participating in sport may result in students' personal and social development, and as a result diminish the incidents of health-compromising behaviors, is based on the tenets of the Olympic ideal-the integration of mind and body (Danish & Nellen, 1997). However, there is nothing about sport itself (the ball, the venue or the equipment) that teaches children how to: concentrate; believe in themselves; believe to their future; and/or become more responsible (Danish, 2001). These skills that integrate mind and body must be taught in conjunction with and through sport. In other words, we must teach "education through the physical" as opposed to "education of the physical". As Siedentop (1980) distinguished these two orientations, the latter has physical fitness as its primary goal; the former has general education as the primary goal. When we adopt an "education through the physical" we are committing ourselves to teaching both physical and mental fitness. We must emphasize the valuable skills and attitudes learned during sport participation and how students can apply these skills to daily life.

Laker (2000) suggests that physical education should no longer be about skill acquisition and performance only. It is an opportunity for physical education to be linked more closely with personal, social, health education and citizenship. The practicalities of such an enterprise will need to be addressed in teacher education program and in teaching in schools. To use physical education to promote personal growth, we first must recognize that physical activity is a metaphor for enhancing competence, not an end in itself. In other words, the lasting value of a sport experience lies in the application of the principles learned through participation and then transferred to other areas.

Petitipas et al. (2005) suggest that positive development can happen when young people are: (a) engaged in a desired activity within an appropriate environment (context); (b) surrounded by caring adult mentors and a positive group or community (external assets); (c) learning to acquire skills (internal assets) that are important for managing life situation; and (d) benefiting from the findings of a comprehensive system of evaluation and research. The question and the challenge for physical educators and coaches is how to test and build on these positive developments in practice.

Hellison (1995) developed a program for teachers and coaches to teach responsibility through physical activity. The model consists of five levels of what it means for A student to be responsible for: (a) respecting the rights and feelings of others; (b) understanding the role of effort in improving oneself in physical activity and life; (c) being self-directed and responsible for one's own well-being; (d) being sensitive and responsible for the well-being of others; and (e) applying what you have learned in different non-physical activity/sport settings. Cummings (1997) examined the impact of the program on school attendance, grades and dropout rates. She found that the control group had a 34% school dropout rate as compared to none in the program group. No differences were found between the groups with respect to school attendance or grades.

Danish et al. (1992a, 1992b) developed the Going for Goal (GOAL) program. GOAL is a 10 –hour, 10-session program taught by carefully selected and well- trained high-school students to middle-school or junior high –school students. The program is designed to teach adolescents a sense of personal control and confidence about their future so that they can make better decisions and ultimately became better citizens. Danish (1997) reported an initial evaluation of GOAL that combined different samples that had received the program at different times. Among the major findings were: (a) participants learned the information the GOAL program taught; (b) they were able to achieve the goals they set; (c) they found the process easier than they expected; and (d) they thought they had learned quite a bit about how to set goals. O' Hearn and Gatz (1999, 2002) conducted two studies using GOAL with mostly Hispanic students. In one study, participating students, compared to a wait – list control group, gained knowledge about the skills being taught and were able to attain the goals they set. In the second study, they also improved their problem solving skills.

Danish (2002) developed a sport–based program that takes advantage of the clearly defined, contingency-dependent, closed environment of sport and uses it as a "training ground" for life. The program is called SUPER (*Sports United to Promote Education and Recreation*) is a sport – based adaptation of the GOAL and its goals are that each participant leave the program with the understanding that: (1) there is a relationship between performance excellence in sport and personal excellence in life; (2) mental skills can enhance both sport performance and personal performance; (3) it is important to set and attain goals in sport and life and (4) roadblocks to goals can be overcome.

SUPER is a peer-led series of 18 modules taught like sports clinics. Participants are involved in three sets of activities: learning the physical skills related to a specific sport; learning life skills related to sports and life in general; and playing the sport. For an extended discussion of the conceptual framework for SUPER, readers are referred to Danish, Forneris, Hodge & Heke (2004) and Danish,Taylor & Fazio (2003). The SUPER Program has been implemented in conjunction with several sports including basketball, soccer, golf, rugby and volleyball. Hodge, Heke, & McCarroll, (2000) applied the SUPER model in the development of the Rugby Advantage Program (RAP) in New Zealand. Danish and his colleagues (Danish, 2001) applied the program to golf.

Papacharisis, Goudas, Danish & Theodorakis (2005) applied an abbreviated (eight sessions) of the program to soccer and volleyball. The design for both studies was a pre-test, post-test comparison group design with the intervention integrated into the teaching of the sports skills and games. The first study involved 40 female volleyball players on two teams; the second study involved 32 male soccer players on two different teams. In each study, one team served as the "experimental" team, the other as the "control" team. In both studies, measures included assessments of physical skills; knowledge of the SUPER program; and self-beliefs about their ability to set goals, to problem solve, and to think positively. The results of both studies indicated that students on the experimental teams indicated higher self-beliefs for personal goal setting, problem solving and positive thinking than did those on the control teams. In addition, students in the intervention demonstrated an increase in program knowledge and improvement in physical skills compared to students in the control condition.

In the current study we sought to extend the results of the above research (Papacharisis et. all. 2005) to a physical education course. The purpose was to examine the effectiveness of the same abbreviated version of SUPER in a physical education setting. We examined the impact the program had on students' knowledge and ability to use life skills, on their performance in sport skill and their sense of self efficacy about their performance. Self-efficacy was defined as the confidence individuals had in their ability to execute a course of action or attain specific performance outcomes (Bandura, 1997).

METHOD

Participants

The study was conducted with classes in elementary school. Participants were 97 (59 boys, 38 girls), all of them were Greek citizens aged 10 – 12 years old ($M = 11.16$ years old, $SD = .64$). The participants were divided into two teams and randomly assigned into an experimental ($n = 48$, 31 boys, 17 girls) and a control ($n = 49$, 28 boys, 21 girls) group.

Description of the Life Skills Program

The program was an abbreviated form of SUPER. The main differences were: (a) the sessions were shorter (8 sessions of 15 minutes); (b) they took place during physical education classes; and (c) the program began with a sport skill test (described below). Test result of the sport skill served as stimuli for pupils to set goals. Learning objectives were introduced in combination with sport practice. The intervention itself included discussion, group learning, and written worksheets.

In the beginning of the program, participants were evaluated on two different sports skills related to the contents of the physical education class. In the first two sessions of the program, in addition to practice, pupils discussed their performance on the test with the physical education teacher, discussed the importance of setting goals, and were asked to set reachable goals to achieve over the two months of practice. In session three, athletes were taught the characteristics of reachable goals (positively stated, specific, important to the goal setter, and under to the goal setter's control). In session four and five, they were taught and practiced setting goals for themselves that were stated positively, specifically, important to them and under their control.. In sessions six and seven, a problem solving technique (STAR) was taught. STAR stands for Stop and take a deep breath, Think of all the alternatives, anticipate the consequences of each choice and Respond with the best choice. They then identified possible roadblocks to reaching their goals and practiced the STAR problem -solving strategy to help them overcome the roadblocks. Finally in session eight, they were taught how to make a plan (or goal ladder) to reach their goal. Participants learned the importance of developing plans to reach goals and made plans to reach the goals they have set.

During the eight sessions, participants had as a reference point their own personal goal that they had to achieve in the particular sport skill. Having this goal in mind, they learned how to think positive, solve problem and make plans to achieve the goal.

Procedure

Prior to the intervention, all participants were asked to complete the questionnaires and performance test. SUPER was then taught to the experimental groups at the beginning of each physical education class for a period of eight weeks. The program was taught by the physical education teacher (one of the experimenters). Concurrently, the same physical education course without the SUPER intervention was taught to the control group. At the end of the eight-week program, all participants completed the questionnaires and performance test for a second time. Data form both teams (Experimental and Control) were collected by the same experimenter.

Instruments

Sport Skills
Participants' performance on physical education was evaluated with a test on basketball chest passes. Participants score was made up by the number of repetitions executed during 30 seconds against a wall two meters away (Barrow, McGee, 1979).

Self-efficacy Test
Self-efficacy was assessed by asking each participant how confident they were regarding their score in basketball test. Participants were asked to rate the strength and magnitude of their self-efficacy expectations for five performance levels: 10, 20, 30, 40, and 50. The format used is comparable to that of Bandura and Jourden (1991) and Theodorakis (1996) studies (e.g. " I can do 20 pass in a row against the wall in 30 seconds" Yes – No) and " How certain you are?" answered in a 10 point scale anchored by "certain" (10) and "uncertain" (1). The strength of self-efficacy was the sum of the certainty scores for the five levels of performance. Cronbach's alpha for this scale was .79.

Knowledge Test
A 10-item multiple – choice test was used to evaluate knowledge of how to set goals, solve problems, and think positively. For example, "In order to make a dream come true: (a) I should dream more and more, (b) I must turn the dream into a goal, (c) I must sit and wait for something to happen, (d) I don't have to do anything. If I want it, it will happen." The instrument was developed and validated for the same ages in our previous studies (Papacharisis et. all, 2005, Papacharisis, 2002).

Self-Beliefs for the Ability of Goal Setting, Problem Solving, and Positive Thinking

A 15-item scale measuring self – beliefs for goal setting, problem solving and positive thinking, based on the work of Papacharisis, Goudas, Danish, and Theodorakis (2005) was administrated. Five items were developed to assess students' perceptions of goal setting (e.g., "I am very good at setting goals for my self"); five items were developed to assess students' perceptions of problem solving ability (e.g., "I am very good at solving problems that I have"); and five items were developed to assess students' perceptions of positive thinking (e.g. "I am very good at thinking positively for myself"). A 7-point scale was used (1= *strongly disagree* to 7 = *strongly agree*). Cronbach's alpha coefficients were: .81 for Goal Setting, .77 for Problem Solving, and .80 for Positive Thinking.

A social desirability scale, the M-C Form A (Reynolds, 1982), was also completed to examine relationships of the questionnaire items with social desirability. The results revealed that the correlations with social desirability were low.

RESULTS

Descriptive statistics were computed for each of the variables for pre-test and post- test and are displayed in Table 1.

Table 1. Descriptive statistics of the study

Variables	Experimental group				Control group			
	Pre		Post		Pre		Post	
	M	SD	M	SD	M	SD	M	SD
Knowledge test	5.02	1.12	7.43	1.90	5.14	1.33	5.22	1.18
Self-beliefs - Goal setting	5.17	.83	5.73	.78	5.20	1.00	5.14	1.02
Self-beliefs - Problem solving	5.04	.74	5.80	.83	5.05	.81	4.93	1.00
Self-beliefs - Positive thinking	4.89	.95	5.67	.87	4.96	.79	4.81	.90
Basketball skill tests - Chest pass	16.87	6.40	23.83	6.20	10.53	5.40	11.37	5.70
Self-efficacy	7.33	1.80	8.78	1.20	6.78	1.80	7.20	1.60

Knowledge Test

A repeated – measure ANOVA with knowledge scores as the dependent variable, time of measurement as the within- subjects factor, and group as the between –subjects factor, revealed a significant Group x Time interaction, $F (1, 94) = 16.78$, $p< .001$, $\eta^2 = .32$. Post hoc analysis revealed that the two groups were not significantly different in their knowledge about life skills before the program, $t (94) = .12$, $p > .01$. By contrast, after the program, the knowledge score of the Experimental group was significantly higher than that of the Control group, $t (94) = 8.07$, $p < .001$.

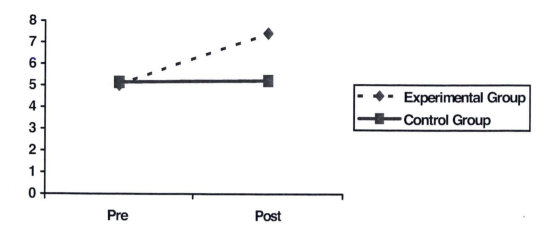

Figure 1. Change in Knowledge Test from pre-test to post test for experimental and control groups.

Self – Beliefs

A repeated – measure MANOVA with Goal Setting, Problem Solving, and Positive thinking as the dependent variables, time of measurement as the within-subject factor and groups as the between subjects factor revealed a significant multivariate group by time interaction, $F (3, 88) = 6.17, p < .001, \eta^2 = .44$. Univariate tests showed significant interaction effects for Goal Setting, $F (1, 93) = 6.78, p < .05, \eta^2 = .33$, Problem Solving, $F (1, 93) = 15.43, p < .001, \eta^2 = .31$, and Positive Thinking, $F (1, 93) = 10.16, p< .01, \eta^2 = .27$. To further investigate the interaction, repeated measures ANOVA'S were performed for each group separately. The analysis revealed that there was a significant improvement for Goal Setting", $F (1, 47) = 15.16, p < .001, \eta^2 = .34$, Problem solving $F (1, 47) = 33.82, p < .001, \eta^2 = .63$ and Positive Thinking, $F (1, 47) = 20.42, p < .01, \eta^2 = 42$. In contrast, there were no significant differences for the control group.

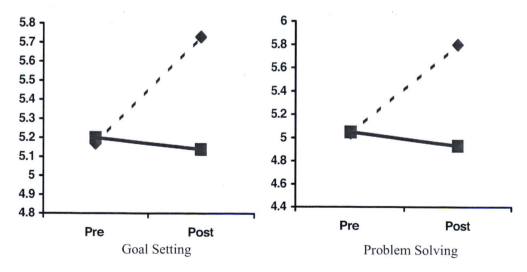

Figure 2. (Continued)

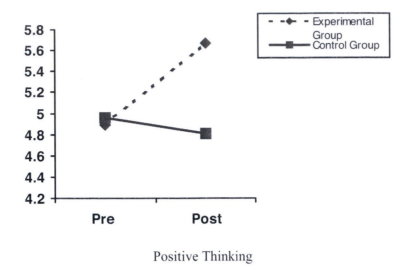

Positive Thinking

Figure 2. Change in Self-Beliefs for the Ability of Goal Setting, Problem Solving, and Positive Thinking from pre-test to post test for experimental and control groups.

Performance Test

A repeated measures ANOVA showed a significant group by time interaction for the basketball skill test, F (1, 94) = 52.95, $p < .001$, $\eta^2 = .73$. To further investigate the interaction, paired samples t-tests were performed for each group separately. The analyses revealed significant improvement for the experimental group, t (47) = 11.32, $p < .001$, whereas no differences were detected for the control group.

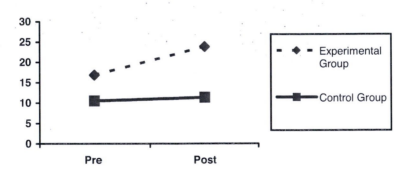

Figure 3. Change in basketball chest passes from pre-test to post test for experimental and control groups.

Self-efficacy

Results of the repeated measures ANOVA showed a significant group by time interaction for self-efficacy score, F (1, 94) = 15.95, $p < .001$, $\eta^2 = .38$. The results indicated that scores of self-efficacy increased significantly for the experimental group t (47) = 7.62, $p < .001$. There were no significant differences for the control group.

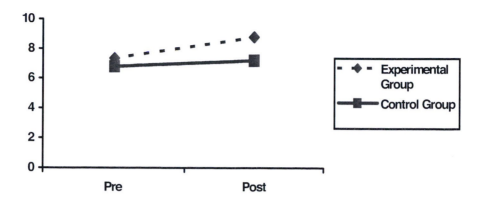

Figure 4. Change in Self- efficacy, from pre-test to post test for experimental and control groups

CONCLUSION

The purpose of the present study was to examine the effectiveness of a life skills program for students through their physical education classes. The program teaches intrapersonal skills including Goal Setting, Problem Solving and Positive Thinking. The aim was to promote, the knowledge of the use of life skills among the students s as well as the acquisition of sports skill and the feelings of self –efficacy.

The results of the program are promising. Students who received the program showed greater improvement regarding their knowledge and their self – beliefs for personal Goal Setting, Problem Solving and Positive Thinking than did students in the control group. In addition, they reported higher score in sport skill test and higher scores in self – efficacy than did students in the control group. Prior research on the application of life skills program in sport setting reported significant changes on participants' knowledge about life skills and perceptions of their ability to achieve the goal they have set (O'Hearn & Gatz 1999; 2002; Papacharisis, et.al., 2005). Brunelle, Danish, and Fazio (2002), have also reported significant changes on social responsibility, emotional intelligence, goal knowledge and social interest, as a result of implementing an abbreviated version of SUPER.

The results denote that when life skills training is appropriately embedded in physical education curriculum, the life skills learned are not at the expense of learning sport skills training. One explanation for these findings may be related to the participatory learning methods used in the program including: hearing an explanation of the skill in question; observing f the skill (modelling); practicing the skill in selected situations in a supportive learning environment; and receiving feedback about individual performance of skills. Practice and the learning of these life skills were facilitated by the practice and performance demands of the sports skills.

The present study had at least two limitations that should be considered when interpreting the results. The first limitation is the lack of follow-up to see whether the intervention had any lasting effects. The second limitation is that much of the outcome data is based on the students' self-reports. Future studies should employ behavioural measures of students use life skills and a longer follow-up period (at least a year). Additional factors may be measured to assess the impact of a life skills programme, such us the effect of life skills education on school performance and school attendance.

A conscious emphasis on using life skills in the context of physical education classes may make programs more effective in achieving their stated goals. Focusing on personal goal setting, problem solving and positive thinking and encouraging students to use these skills can result in improved skill and fitness, in addition to greater knowledge. By designing activities that truly promote elements and knowledge that are necessary for successfully coping with the complex realities of life, we can hopefully influence our students' lives "beyond the physical".

REFERENCES

Bandura, A. (1977). *Social learning theory.* Englewood Cliffs, NJ: Prentice-Hall.

Bandura, A., & Jourden, F. (1991). Self-regulatory mechanisms governing the impact of social comparison on complex decision making. *Journal of Personality & Social Psychology, 45,* 191-215

Brunelle, J., Danish, S.J., & Fazio, R.(2002). *The impact of a sport-based community project on adolescent volunteers prosocial values.* Unpublised manuscript.

Barrow, H. M., & McGee, R. (1979). *A practical approach to measurement in physical education.* Philadelphia: Lea & Febiger.

Cummings, T. (1997). *Testing the effectiveness of Hellison's Personal and Social Responsibility Model.* Unpublished Master's thesis, California State University, Chico.

Danish, S.J., Forneris, T., Hodge, K., Heke, I. (2004). Enhancing youth development through sport. *World Leisure, 46* (3), 38-49.

Danish, S.J., Taylor, T., Fazio, R. (2003). Enhancing adolescent development through sport and leisure. (pp. 92-108).In G.R. Adams & M. Berzonsky (Eds.), *Blackwell Handbook on Adolescence.* Malden, MA: Blackwell.

Danish, S.J. (2002). *SUPER (Sports united to promote education and recreation) program: Leader manual and student activity book.* (3rd Edition). Richmond, VA: Life Skills Center, Virginia Commonwealth University.

Danish, S.J. (2001). The First Tee: Teaching youth to succeed in golf and in life. In P.R. Thomas (Ed.), *Optimistic performance in golf* (pp. 67-74). Brisbane, Australia: Australian Academic Press.

Danish, S.J., (1997). Going for the Goal: A life skills program for adolescents. In Gullota, T. & Albee, G. (Eds.) *Primary Prevention Works* (pp. 291-312). Newbury Park: Sage.

Danish, S. J., & Nellen, C. V. (1997). New roles for sport psychologist: Teaching life skills through sport to at-risk youth. *QUEST, 49,* 100-113.

Danish, S., Petitpas, A., & Hale, B. (1995). Psychological innervations: A life development model. In S. M. Murphy (Ed.), *Sport psychology interventions* (pp.11-38). Champaign, IL: Human Kinetics Danish, S. J., Mash, J. M., Howard, C.W., Curl, S.J., Meyer, A.L., Owens, S., et al.(1992 a). *Going for the goal leader manual.* Richmond VA: Department of Psychology, Virginia Commonwealth University.

Danish, S. J., Mash, J. M., Howard, C.W., Curl, S.J., Meyer, A.L., Owens, S., et al.(1992 b). *Going for the goal student activity manual.* Richmond VA: Department of Psychology, Virginia Commonwealth University.

Helisson, D. (1995). *Teaching responsibility through physical activity.* Champaing, IL: Human Kinetics

Hodge, K., Heke, J.I., & McCarroll, N. (2000). *The Rugby Advantage Program (RAP)* Unpublised manuscript, University of Otago, Dunedin, New Zealand.

Laker, A. (2000). *Beyond the boundaries of physical education.* London: Routledge Falmer Taylor & Francis Group.

O'Hearn, T. C., & Gatz, M. (1999). Evaluating a psychological competence program for urban adolescents. *Journal of Prevation,20,* 119-144.

O'Hearn, T. C., & Gatz, M. (2002). Going for the goal: Improving youth problem solving skills through a school-based intervention. *Journal of Community Psychology, 30,* 281-303.

Papacharisis, V. (2002) *Implementation of a life skills development program in physical education and sports.* Unpublished doctorate dissertation, University of Thessaly, Greece.

Papacharisis, V., Goudas, M., Danis, S. J., & Theodorakis, Y. (2005). The effectiveness of teaching life skills program in a sport context. *Journal of Applied Sport Psychology, 17,* 247- 254.

Petitpas, A., Cornelius, A., Van Raalte, J., Jones, T. (2005). A framework for planning youth sport programs that foster psychological development. *The Sport Psycologist, 19,* 63-80.

Reynolds, W. M. (1982). Development of reliable and valid short forms of the Marlow-Crowe Social Desirability Scale. *Journal of Clinical Psychology, 38,* 119-125.

Siedentop, D. (1980). *Physical education: Introductory analysis.* Dubuque, Iowa: William C. Brown.

Theodorakis, Y. (1996). The influence of goals, commitment, self-efficacy and self-satisfaction on motor performance. *Journal of Applied Sport Psychology,8,* 171- 182.

World Health Organization. (1999). *Partners in life skills education.*Geneva, Switzerland: World Health Organization, Department of Mental Health.

In: Motivation of Exercise and Physical Activity
Editor: Liam A. Chiang, pp. 79-91

ISBN: 978-1-60021-596-4
© 2007 Nova Science Publishers, Inc.

Chapter 6

Choice Behavior Expressed in Elite Sport Competition: Predicting Shot Selection and Game Outcomes in College Basketball

Jennifer L. Hitt, Larry A. Alferink, Thomas S. Critchfield and Jeffrey B. Wagman
Illinois State University, USA

Abstract

Coaches and fans alike know that a key factor in athletic team success is player motivation to perform well in game situations. For instance, basketball players must decide which shots to take and make wise decisions when they do so. The present study applied operant choice theory to understanding one facet of this decision. Operant choice theory addresses the problem of how individuals decide to distribute limited time and effort among mutually exclusive potential courses of action. The core assumption is that they do so based on expected consequences (in generic terms, reinforcement and punishment) associated with these actions. In the present study, we predicted shot selection (two-point versus three-point field goals) by players on eleven teams in a major college conference using a mathematical model of operant choice. Specifically, each player's ratio of two-point to three-point shots attempted was predicted as a function of the ratio of two-point to three-point shots made. This analysis is interesting in two respects. First, many people assume that operant principles, which have often been derived from research on nonhumans, have little to say about complex human behavior. Second, few kinds of behavior are as complex as those involved in elite sport competition, where a host of factors that are not included in our mathematical model are thought to apply. Nevertheless, our results strongly suggest that the choices players make are motivated by reinforcement. The choices players make are quite sensitive to the reinforcement for those choices and the model predicted most of the variance in shot selection among the players on each team. Whether shot selection contributes meaningfully to team success was considered in a follow-up analysis that used model fits to predict the winners of games in the season-ending league tournament. Overall, these results illustrate the broad generality of operant principles to everyday situations and suggests that these principles are quite robust in motivating behavior even in situations that are far more complex and dynamic than those studied in the laboratory.

INTRODUCTION

Two high-caliber teams are playing basketball. One team's star guard dribbles the ball down the court, and detects two opportunities simultaneously: an opening through which he might drive for a two-point lay-up, and an open area, further away from the basket, from which he might launch a three-point shot. Which shot does he take?

Traditional discussions of sport performance might invoke two grounds upon which to speculate what happens next. First, the guard's choice of shots might be dictated by the dynamic features of the game -- the current score, time left on the clock, his level of fatigue, the other players with whom he currently shares the court, and so on. In the context of such variables, no two moments of competition are identical, in which case successful performance depends on the player's ability to think wisely about complex circumstances. Second, the guard's choice of shots might be assumed to reflect fairly stable personality factors. Some players, for example, are risk takers, who would be expected to prefer three-point shots that can generate points quickly but are hard to make. Others are more conservative by nature, and thus would be expected to prefer the safer, though less lucrative, two-point lay-up.

Importantly, in considering what motivates athlete choices among incompatible courses of action, the perspectives just described share a common theme: Both cognitive ability and temperament are individual-differences variables. Rarely mentioned in analyses of sport behavior are the general-process variables that are stressed in many empirical accounts of learning and motivation. Yet if these variables are as general as they appear to be across laboratory experiments, they should also manifest in natural environments. With this in mind, the present analysis explores the applicability of a well-understood behavior principle to shot selection in basketball. Although the analysis is incapable of predicting what a given player will do at a given moment, across games, moments, and players -- which clearly vary along many dimensions -- it reveals a recurring pattern that is remarkably consistent with what individuals do in controlled laboratory studies.

Shot selection in basketball is a choice between two mutually-exclusive alternatives. This kind of choice is often studied in the laboratory using an arrangement analogous to that shown in Figure 1. The subject, here a pigeon, may divide limited time and effort between two (or more) courses of action, represented by pecking either of two lighted disks. Among the factors known to influence this division of labor is the consequence of each action -- for laboratory convenience, this may be manipulated in terms of how often pecking each disk yields access to food reinforcement, and in what amount. Herrnstein (1961) showed that the effort invested in each alternative was proportional to the reinforcement for that alternative. This relationship can be described mathematically as

$$\frac{B_1}{B_1 + B_2} = \frac{r_1}{r_1 + r_2} \tag{1}$$

with B terms representing rates of responding to alternatives 1 and 2, and r terms representing the reinforcement that depends on this responding. Only a little imagination is required to envision two-point and three-point shots as behavior alternatives in this formulation, and shots made as reinforcement for these attempts. Thus, it may be predicted that, although many other factors clearly influence basketball performance, a player's probability of taking two-point versus three-point shots will reflect the likelihood of making those shots.

Figure 1. A common preparation for examining choice in the laboratory. The subject, a pigeon, must distribute limited time and effort between two behavior alternatives, pecking either of two response keys. Each course of action occasionally yields reinforcement in the form of food delivered through the rectangular aperture.

The relation suggested in Equation 1 is, in contemporary terms, commonly expressed in the form of Baum's (1974) generalized matching equation

$$\log(B_1 / B_2) = a \log(r_1 / r_2) + \log k \tag{2}$$

As in Equation 1, B_1 and B_2 represent the rates of responding for each response alternative and the rates of reinforcement for those alternatives are represented by r_1 and r_2 respectively. Logarithmic transformations in Equation 2 allow the relationship between behavior and reinforcement to be described by a straight line, the y-intercept of which, k, is a measure of bias, or preference for one alternative irrespective of the reinforcement availability measured in r terms. Bias can occur for a variety of reasons such as one alternative requiring more effort, or, relevant to the present analysis, a difference in either the quality or quantity of reinforcement. The slope of the line, a, is regarded as a measure of how sensitive behavior is to discrepancies in reinforcement frequency. When the ratio of the two behaviors varies perfectly with the ratio of reinforcement, $a = 1.0$, representing perfect *matching* of effort allocation to reinforcement frequency. When $a < 1.0$ (*undermatching*), behavior allocation changes proportionally less across circumstances than reinforcement frequency. In the extreme case ($a = 0$) the individual behaves as if the two response alternatives always yield identical reinforcement. When $a > 1.0$, behavior allocation changes proportionally more across circumstances than reinforcement frequency.

Close approximations of the matching law's predictions have been observed under a number of laboratory and real-world situations. For example, in school classrooms, the prevalence of appropriate versus inappropriate student behavior reliably tracks the relative likelihood that teacher attention is forthcoming following them (Martens, Halperin, Rummel, & Kilpatrick, 1990). There is also reason to expect the matching law to be expressed in athletic performance in sporting events. Reed, Critchfield, and Martens (2006) examined the selection of passing vs. rushing plays by coaches of professional NFL football teams. With yards gained as a metric of reinforcement for play calling, Equation 2 accounted for a median of about 60% of the variance in play calling across the 32 NFL teams.

Similarly, Vollmer and Bourret (2000) examined two-point vs. three-point shot selection by players on two college basketball teams, using shots made as a measure of reinforcement. They found that shot selection closely followed the predictions of Equation 1, although the study was narrow in scope. Specifically, the data were from successful men's and women's teams at a single institution. It is not clear whether the matching law would as effectively describe the performances of other teams, including less successful ones.

The present study tested the generality of Vollmer and Bourret's (2000) findings by examining shot selection during 2006 by players on the 11 men's basketball teams of the Big Ten Conference, a coalition of Division I National Collegiate Athletic Association schools. Table 1 shows that season won-loss records ranged from Ohio State University's .813 (.750 in Big Tem conferences games) to Purdue University's .321 (.183 in conference games). Thus, we were able to evaluate matching law predictions for players on teams of varying abilities. In addition, since shot selection is widely regarded as an important component of basketball offense, and offense is an important factor in the outcome of basketball games, we examined the relationship between team matching during the regular season and outcomes of games in the conference's annual championship tournament.

METHOD

Season-aggregate statistics for players on each of the 11 conference teams were obtained from electronic archives (downloaded between March and September, 2006, from http://www. espn.com). To be included in the analyses, an individual player must have attempted at least 15 two-point shots and 15 three-point shots over the course of the season and made a minimum of one two-point and one three-point basket. These criteria were chosen to avoid zero values, which cannot be accommodated in ratio-based analyses, but necessarily meant that a few players could not be evaluated.

For each eligible player, two ratios were computed. The first, representing behavior allocation, was the log of the ratio of two-point shot attempts over three-point shot attempts. The second, representing reinforcement, was the log of the ratio of two-point shots made over three-point shots made. Together, these two ratios yielded one data point per player. This approach differs from that normally taken in the laboratory, where the matching law is a description of individual behavior. Typically, Equation 2 is fit to data from a single individual performing in multiple conditions in which reinforcement values for competing actions vary. It appears, however, that the relation also is fairly robust in describing the pooled data from many individuals (Gray, Stafford, & Tallman, 1991; Reed, et al, 2006). Thus, in their seminal basketball study, Vollmer and Bourret (2000) described matching in the aggregate player data of individual teams. Their approach was replicated here, with generalized matching relation expressed as

$$\log\left(\frac{2attempt}{3attempt}\right) = a\log\left(\frac{2made}{3made}\right) + \log k \tag{3}$$

and fit to each team's data via least-squares linear regression.

Fitting Equation 3 to a team's data yielded three dependent measures: the percentage of variance accounted for by the regression line, which is an estimate of how well the equation describes the data; a (slope, or sensitivity to reinforcement-frequency differentials), and $\log k$ (y-intercept, or bias). The last measure bears special explanation. When, as in the case of the two kinds of basketball shots, concurrently available reinforcers differ in size, bias (shifts in the y-intercept, or $\log k$) has been shown to result (Landon, Davison, and Elliffe, 2003). Thus, $\log k$ provides an empirical measure of the extent to which reinforcer size, a potent motivational variable, influences choice. In the Vollmer and Bourret (2000) study, however, a statistical adjustment for the differential value of two-point and three-point baskets was employed that may have neutralized this potentially interesting effect. For the purposes of the present study, no such adjustment was made, allowing $\log k$ to serve as a measure of the extent to which, for each team, differential point values influenced shot selection. In the context of Equation 2, a positive $\log k$ indicates a bias for two-point shots, and a negative $\log k$ indicates a bias for three-point shots.

RESULTS

Figure 2 summarizes the results of fitting Equation 3 to the data of each of the teams in the Big Ten conference. Within each panel, each data point corresponds to the shot selection of an individual player over the regular season. Also shown is the line of best fit as determined by least squares linear regression. Note that, for each team, data points are clustered closely around the regression line. The bottom, right panel shows a composite analysis incorporating all eligible players from all teams. Three outcomes that are representative of the league as whole may be observed: (1) the GML accounts for most of the variance in shot selection; (2) the slope (a) of the function is less than 1 (undermatching), suggesting less than optimal sensitivity of shot selection to reinforcement frequency differentials; and (3) log y-intercept (*log* k) is negative, indicating a bias for taking three-point shots, as expected based on its higher point value.

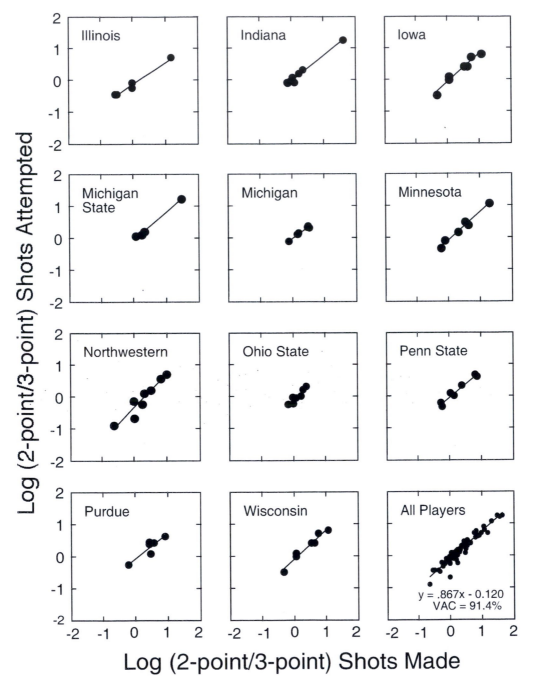

Figure 2. Least squares linear regression fit of Equation 3 to shot selection by each of the eleven teams in the Big Ten Conference during the regular season and to players on all eleven teams included in the analysis.

Table 1. Summary of Tournament Teams

Team	Slope	Bias	%Vact	# Players Inc.	Win-Loss Record[a]
Illinois	0.688	-0.150	97.9	5	26-7 (11-5)
Indiana	0.782	-0.043	97.9	8	19-12 (9-7)
Iowa	1.014	-0.161	95.1	6	25-9 (11-5)
Michigan	0.723	-0.045	97.2	7	22-11 (8-8)
Michigan State	0.873	-0.067	99.3	4	22-12 (8-8)
Minnesota	0.876	-0.101	97.8	6	16-15 (5-11)
Northwestern	1.037	-0.340	90.5	8	14-15 (6-10)
Ohio State	0.939	-0.132	85.1	7	26-6 (12-4)
Penn State	0.812	-0.062	95.8	7	15-15 (6-10)
Purdue	0.788	-0.085	81.3	6	9-19 (3-13)
Wisconsin	0.892	-0.101	95.7	7	19-12 (9-7)

[a] Overall win-loss record (Conference win-loss record).

For all individual teams (Table 1), the GML accounted for at least four-fifths of the variance in shot selection (median = 95.8%). Most teams undermatched, although sensitivity to reinforcement (slope; a) varied considerably across teams, ranging from .688 to 1.037 (median = .873). Every team exhibited a bias for three-point shots (range = -.043 to -.340; median = -.101).

CONCLUSION

Consistency with other GML Findings

Decisions made in complex everyday environments, including those in sport competition, often are considered without attention to the motivational properties of consequences experienced during the individual's history of making similar choices. The present study confirms and extends the results of Vollmer and Bourret (2000) by showing that the GML, which explicitly invokes history of reinforcement in predicting choice, provided an excellent account of shot selection by players on college basketball teams. Vollmer and Bourret provided only graphic summaries of GML fits, so, to allow comparison with our data, we fit Equation 3 to their raw data (Table 1 of the original article), and found that it accounted for 94.9% and 99.8% of variance for the two teams. In the present analysis, the GML accounted for at least 95% of the variance for 8 of 11 teams. These fits also compare favorably with other naturalistic analyses involving the GML. For example, Martens, et al. (1990) found that the GML accounted for slightly less than half of the variance in childrens' classroom behavior as a function of teacher attention. Reed et al. (2006) found that the GML accounted for a median of 60% of the variance in play calling by the offensive coordinators of 32 NFL football teams. Better fits were obtained for every team in the present analysis.

Most teams in the present study showed undermatching, thereby replicating the normative finding in laboratory studies of choice by individuals (e.g. Baum, 1979; Robinson, 1992), and in Reed et al's study of play calling in professional football (median slope = 0.575 for 32 NFL offensive coordinators). Our re-analysis of data from Vollmer and Bourret (2000) revealed slopes of 0.913 and 1.045 for their two teams. The present study, though limited in scope, suggests that those values may be at the upper end of the distribution for college basketball teams.

Finally, all teams in the present study exhibited a bias towards taking three-point shots irrespective of reinforcement frequency, and outcomes that also appeared in our re-analysis of the Vollmer and Bourret (2000) data (1.137 and -.097). Given the higher point value associated with these shots, the finding is in keeping with laboratory research showing biases generated by higher-magnitude reinforcement (Landon et al., 2003).

Despite the close correspondence of the present findings with those of laboratory experiments on choice, the parallels between laboratory contingencies and those operating in basketball should not be overstated. In the laboratory, matching typically is studied in the context of concurrent variable-interval (VI) reinforcement schedules (e.g. Herrnstein, 1961), in which the first response after an unpredictable time period elapses yields reinforcement. These reinforcement schedules are employed, not to mimic everyday situations, but rather to isolate factors (such as the role of time) that operate in everyday contingencies (Chance, 2003). Not surprisingly, the "reinforcement schedules" of basketball are, as Vollmer and Bourret (2000) observed, only loosely related to those of the typical matching experiment. In both cases, of course, only a subset of criterion responses yield reinforcement. In the laboratory, opportunities to make criterion responses are freely available, while in basketball a player can only shoot with possession of the ball. Even with possession, a player may not find defenders in a position that readily accommodates shooting, or may be assigned by a coach's plan to get the ball into a teammate's possession. Thus, most possessions end with a pass to another player rather than a shot opportunity. Unfortunately, for analytical purposes, the interval-like and non-interval-like properties of basketball scoring contingencies are impossible to disentangle. It should be noted that, in the laboratory, the matching law sometimes has difficulty accounting for performance under non-interval schedules (e.g. Herrnstein and Loveland, 1975). Thus, the complex contingencies of basketball competition might be expected to create relatively poor fits of the matching law to shot selection. In this context, the matching law's success in accounting for shot selection seems quite remarkable.

Whatever the successes of the present analysis, it examined only teams playing in the upper echelon of collegiate conferences. For example, in 2006, 6 of 11 Big Ten schools were invited to participate in the NCAA Division I championship tournament, and 3 additional teams participated in the National Invitational Tournament. Overall, the conference was ranked first out of 32 NCAA Division I conferences by the Rating Percentage Index (RPI), a commonly cited collegiate basketball ratings service (http://rpiratings.com). The same may be said of the two teams examined by Vollmer and Bourret (2000), both of which were among the nation's most successful in the year under consideration. Further analyses are needed to see whether the matching law also predicts shot selection at other levels of play.

Shot Selection and Team Success: Preliminary Evaluations

To the extent that shot selection matters in basketball, a matching law account of shot selection should predict face-valid outcomes such as team success. Reed et al. (2006), for example, found that a National Football league team's sensitivity to reinforcement differentials was a modest, but statistically significant, predictor of season winning percentage. The present study incorporated too few teams to support the same analysis, but we have conducted a conducted a larger study involving the 30 top-ranked and 30 bottom-ranked Division I college basketball teams in 2004 (Hitt, Critchfield, and Alferink, 2007). We found that highly-ranked teams exhibited steeper slopes in the matching relation and had more pronounced bias for three-point shots. In general, the GML accounted for more variance in the shot selection on these teams.

As a preliminary extension of the present study, we sought to evaluate whether GML outcomes, based on season-aggregate data, would be useful in predicting the winners of conference tournament games. Pairings and game scores were obtained from http://wwwbigten.com, and the slope of each team's regression line was used to predict outcomes in the 10 tournament games. Winners of each game were predicted by selecting the team with the most optimal sensitivity to reinforcement, that is, with slope (a) closest to 1.0.

Although the slope, bias, and variance accounted for by the GML were computed for all teams, only the slope was used in this preliminary exercise because shot selection is so often described by basketball observers as critically important to a team's success, and the slope of the matching function defines shot selection in terms of a generic motivational variable, reinforcement sensitivity. Moreover, pilot analyses provided limited encouragement that bias (log k) and percent variance accounted for were associated with game outcomes.

Figure 3 shows the tournament bracket. Each team's tournament seeding is indicated along with its GML equation (including, most notably, the slope, a), reproduced from Table 1. For each game, a team's point total is shown in parentheses, and the victorious team is shown in boldface. Winners with the more optimal slope are underlined; otherwise the winner is italicized. In 8 of 10 games, winners had slopes closer to perfect matching than their opponents. This outcome bordered on statistical significance according to the binomial probability test (one tailed), with $p = .055$.

The present analysis is encouraging, but limited in two important ways. First, the number of games involved was small, and bears replicating with a much larger sample. Second, predictions were based on raw differences in slope, meaning that, in principle, a winner could be predicted on the basis of as little as one one-thousandth of a slope unit. This raises the question of what constitutes a meaningful difference in reinforcement sensitivity. One approach would be to define teams as different if their slopes diverged by at least one standard deviation in the distribution of slopes under consideration (0.112 slope units in the present study), and to forego predictions when team slopes are too similar. This more conservative approach would have invalidated 3 of 10 games from our pilot exercise, and thus can only be applied with a larger sample of games.

An additional factor that could have an impact on the predictive accuracy of a GML account is the inclusion criteria used to determine which players enter into a team's analyses. To be subsumed by Equation 3, a player must have taken and made enough two-point and three-point shots to generate a representative sample of behavior. Moreover, ratio-based analyses become volatile with small numbers, and, with logarithmic transformations, are impossible with zero values. Thus, some players were necessarily excluded from the analyses of several teams. Vollmer and Bourret (2000) used a different criterion (including any player who had taken at least 100 shots total, two-point and three-point attempts combined), but also excluded players.

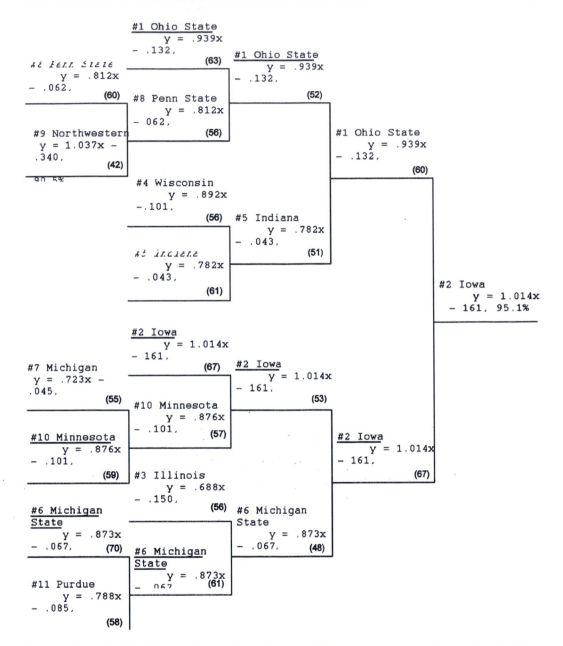

Figure 3. The 2006 Big Ten Conference Men's Basketball Tournament bracket. See text for details.

In some cases, an excluded player has participated little during the season; such exclusions seemed conceptually justified and probably have little effect on the relation between GML outcomes and team success. In other cases, however, mathematically-sensible exclusions remove meaningful data from a team's aggregate. For example, during 2006, Ohio State University's leading scorer, Terrence Dials, took more than 300 shots, and totaled nearly 500 points, without making a single three-point shot, thereby precluding analysis according to Equation 3. Thus, though Dials clearly was a major contributor to Ohio State's noteworthy season, he is not reflected in the present analyses.

A goal of future studies should be to compare different inclusion criteria to see whether this affects the GML's predictive accuracy. The fact is, however, that *any* criterion that meets the mathematical requirements of a ratio-based analysis is destined to exclude players, especially in a sport where some key players (e.g., most centers) rarely take three-point shots. Thus, a GML-based model will not tap all offensive production, and this is likely to limit the model's capacity to predict game outcomes. Another matter to contend with is that idiosyncratic things may occur in a single game (e.g., key player is ill, a noisy home crowd exerts unusual influence, etc.). The single-elimination format of the Big Ten tournament, therefore, might not be the best test of probabilistic relationships such as the one that may exist between victories and matching in shot selection. A better test might occur in a playoff format like that used in the National Basketball Association, which requires a team to win the majority of seven games before moving on to face the next opponent.

Concluding Observations

What determines whether a player, at any given moment, takes a two-point or three-point shot? No analysis of which we are aware can answer this question directly, but at a probabilistic level, the present study demonstrates that a history of reinforcement (in the form of shots made) probably contributes to such decisions over time. Vollmer and Bourret (2000) showed exactly this effect, in fact, by showing that, for most players on the teams they evaluated, shot selection corresponded increasingly closely to GML predictions as the season progressed. Thus, the more elaborate the reinforcement history, the more optimal the shot selection.

Obviously the present analysis ignores much of what is important in basketball success, including defensive abilities of the opposing team. We are unable to ascertain an obvious way to quantify defensive actions in the terms of the matching law. A matching analysis does, however, implicitly account for how well one team adjusts to the defensive efforts of an opponent. Common sense suggests that, across and within games, a player must adjust to variations in opposing team defensive efforts. Such local effects presumably contribute to, but cannot be discerned in, the aggregate analysis of the present study. Thus, a player who adjusts well will show good sensitivity to reinforcement differentials (consistent with a steep slope). One who does not adjust will take, and miss, shots that are not suitable to the situation, and thereby demonstrate poor sensitivity to reinforcement differentials (consistent with a flatter slope).

Unfortunately, an analysis that pools data from several players on a team does not directly illuminate individual reinforcement sensitivity. To do this, a study would need to evaluate individual shot selection under a variety of situations defined by defensive schemes that alter the relative fruitfulness of taking two-point versus three-point shots. For example, opposing teams probably differ in their ability to defend against the two kinds of shots. In this sense, each game might be thought of as a different "experimental condition," in theory allowing shot-selection matching to be studied at the level of the individual player (e.g., see Reed et al., 2006). Unfortunately, for most players a single game provides too few shot opportunities to evaluate according to the conventions of the present analysis. Professional basketball seasons, however, are longer than those in college, and each team plays most opponents several times. Thus, it might be possible to evaluate shot-selection matching for individual professional players by considering each opposing team as an "experimental condition." This would more precisely describe adjustments to changing defensive situations that are merely implied in the present analysis.

Limitations of the present analysis should not overshadow its success in accounting for a critical aspect of elite sport performance *without* invoking the dynamic situational factors or personality variables that dominate discussions about sport. Such factors undoubtedly matter in sport, although it is possible to overestimate their importance. Indeed, lay interpretations of important events, in history as well as in sport, tend to focus on the wisdom or character of individuals, and to ignore powerful, though perhaps unexotic, situational factors (Boring, 1950; Diamond, 1999). In this sense, the present study may appear to run counter to most traditional conceptions of sport, but this is not entirely true. Nothing is more axiomatic to sport than the notion that great athletes are motivated by success. By placing the decision-making of shot selection in a motivational context framed by past reinforcement, the present analysis endorses exactly this perspective, albeit potentially for all athletes, not just exceptional ones.

REFERENCES

Baum, W.M. (1974). On two types of deviation from the matching law: Bias and undermatching. *Journal of the Experimental Analysis of Behavior, 22*, 231-242.

Baum, W.M. (1979). Matching, undermatching, and overmatching in studies of choice. *Journal of the Experimental Analysis of Behavior. 32*, 269-281.

Boring, E.G. (1950). *A history of experimental psychology* (2nd ed.). New York: Appleton.

Chance, P. (2003). Learning and behavior (5th ed.). Pacific Grove, CA: Brooks/Cole.

Diamond, J. (1999). *Guns, germs, and steel*. New York: Norton.

Herrnstein, R.J. (1961). Relative and absolute strength of response as a function of frequency of reinforcement. *Journal of the Experimental Analysis of Behavior, 4*, 267- 272.

Gray, L.N., Stafford, M.C., & Tallman, I. (1991). Rewards and punishment in complex human choices. *Social Psychology Quarterly, 54*, 318-329.

Herrnstein, R.J., & Loveland, D.H. (1975). Maximizing and matching on concurrent ratio schedules. *Journal of the Experimental Analysis of Behavior, 24*, 107-116.

Hitt, J., Critchfield, T.S., & Alferink, L.A. (2007, May). *The matching law and Division I basketball*. Poster presented at the annual meeting of the Association for Behavior Analysis, International, San Diego, CA.

Landon, J., Davison, M., & Elliffe, D. (2003). Concurrent schedules: Reinforcement magnitude effects. *Journal of the Experimental Analysis of Behavior, 79*, 351-365.

Martens, B.K., Halperin, S., Rummel, J., & Kilpatrick, D. (1990). Matching theory applied to contingent teacher attention. *Behavioral Assessment, 12,* 139-155.

Reed, D.D., Critchfield, T.S., & Martens, B.K. (2006). The generalized matching law in elite sport competition: Football play calling as operant choice. *Journal of Applied Behavior Analysis, 39*, 281-297.

Robinson, J.K. (1992). Quantitative analyses of choice in the rat and pigeon. *The Psychological Record, 42*, 437-446.

Vollmer, T.R., & Bourret, J. (2000). An application of the matching law to evaluate the allocation of two-and three- point shots by college basketball players. *Journal of Applied Behavior Analysis, 33,* 137-150.

In: Motivation of Exercise and Physical Activity
Editor: Liam A. Chiang, pp. 93-103

ISBN: 978-1-60021-596-4
© 2007 Nova Science Publishers, Inc.

Chapter 7

COACHING, PARENTING, AND COHESION IN ICE HOCKEY

Birgitta Juntumaa and Marko Elovainio
Department of Psychology, University of Helsinki, Finland

ABSTRACT

This study examined whether similarities or differences between coaching and parenting behaviours are associated with cohesion in sport. The participants were Finnish ice hockey players of 14 and 16 years of age (N=1018) and their parents (N=979). The players rated their coaches using the Leadership Scale of Sport (LSS, Chelladurai & Saleh, 1980) and estimated team cohesion using a four-item scale that was prepared for the present study. Parents rated their own parenting behaviour using the Block's Child Rearing Practices Report (CRPR, Pulkkinen, 1996). Results revealed the importance of matching coaching and parenting that were associated with cohesion. In particular, the compensating combination of Non-Demanding styles at home and high support by the positive coach was associated with high cohesion. These results contribute to our understanding of the important relationship between, coach, parents and player, influencing cohesion and thus motivation at sport. This study is of relevance to coaches, teachers, and parents of young athletes.

Keywords: coaching, parenting, cohesion, motivation, ice hockey

INTRODUCTION

Ice hockey, as a team sport, potentially develops adolescents' physical and social skills. Sport enhances self-esteem, positive body image, and leadership abilities (Barnett, Smoll, & Smith, 1992; Dobosz & Beauty, 1999; Salokun, 1990). Positive coaching behaviour enhances both the satisfaction of players, motivation, and team cohesion (Chelladurai, 1981; Hastie, 1995; Schliesman, 1987). Similarly, the quality of parenting has been shown to be associated with adolescents' well-being, school achievement, and social competence (Aunola, Stattin & Nurmi, 2000; Baumrind, 1991). Little is known, however, about the compatibility between coaching and parenting styles in relation to young players' perception of cohesion in teams. The relationship between the perception of coaching behaviour and its association with cohesion may be dependent on the typical behaviour pattern of the parents.

The Finnish Ice Hockey Association had over 60,000 members in the year 2000. Ice hockey has been very popular especially among boys until the age of 14. Although it is normal to have both sexes in studies about parenting and coaching, we selected only male players, because ice hockey is not as popular among girls in Finland, and we had to consider the issues of being able to generalise our findings.

Leadership styles influence the cohesiveness of the group. A democratic leader facilitates the development of an efficient team, and encourages participation, and thus, enhances the cohesiveness of the group (Muchinsky, 2003). On the contrary, an autocratic leader stifles group cohesiveness (White & Lippitt, 1968); and in sport an autocratic coaching is associated with low group cohesion (Gardner, Shields, Bredemeier & Bostrom, 1996; Hastie, 1995; Weiss & Friedrichs, 1986). Coach leadership is also defined as coaches' behavioural processes that influence team members toward a good performance (Chelladurai & Riemer, 1998), which further motivates team members to stay.

COHESION

Although individual involvement in ice hockey leads boys to stay, the membership of an ice hockey team appears to satisfy many developmental needs of a player, both physical and social, and thus, reflect the elements of cohesion. Research has revealed that both task cohesion (cooperation to achieve common performance goals) and social cohesion (mutual liking, respect, trust) are important elements of cohesion. They are both associated with perception of coach leadership (Carron & Hausenblas, 1998). In fact, coaches who were perceived as high in training and instruction, social support, positive feedback, and democratic behaviours had teams who displayed more cohesive task-related variables. Social cohesion was linked both to social support, and training and instruction behaviours (Gardner, Shields, Bredemeier & Bostrom, 1996; Westre and Weiss, 1991). In summary coaches are able to influence both social and task cohesion at sport with nearly identical leadership behaviours, therefore we use one measure to cover the team cohesion (cooperation and mutual trust).

COACHING BEHAVIOUR

Chelladurai and Saleh (1980) identify five leadership dimensions of coaches' behaviours. *Democratic* coaches allow the team players to participate in decisions concerning the team's goals, methods and strategies, whereas *Autocratic* coaching stresses the leader's personal authority and decision-making, independent of team input. *Training and Instructing* focuses on promoting the players' technical skills and is task-oriented, while the *Social Support* dimension deals with players' emotional and social needs. Coaches exhibiting high Social Support behaviour create a climate that enhances players' mutual satisfaction, warm interpersonal relations, and welfare. *Positive Feedback* -behaviour depends on the athlete's performance but coaches who use it are usually supportive, finding something to praise.

Previous research has revealed that athletes, both boys and girls were most satisfied with coaches whose style involved high levels of Training and Instruction, Democratic style, Social Support and Positive Feedback, and whose style was low in Autocratic coaching behaviour (Hastie, 1995; Weiss & Friedrichs, 1986). The teams of such coaches were also highly cohesive, showing the importance of coaching style for developing team unity (Gardner, Shields, Bredemeier & Bostrom, 1996).

Based on existing research about satisfaction and cohesion, we call the four leadership dimensions, which improve cohesion," Positive Coaching" behaviour. Because autocratic style has found to be associated with lower team cohesion we keep it separate.·

PARENTING TYPOLOGIES

We used child-rearing patterns based on two parenting dimensions described by Maccoby & Martin (1983). *Demanding* parents show control over, demand maturity from, and actively supervise the activities of their children. *Responsive* parents, in contrast, show warmth, acceptance and involvement (Aunola et al., 2000; Barber, 1996).

Democratic (also called 'authoritative') parents are both demanding and responsive. They support autonomous behaviour and provide positive feedback concerning the competence the child wants to achieve. Children of democratic parents have persistence and optimism and a feeling that they have personal control over situations, are socially responsible, develop self-reliance, intrinsic motivations; accomplish high in school, and are well adjusted (Aunola et al., 2000; Barber, 1996). Authoritarian parents show a low level of responsiveness and are highly demanding even punitive. This parent-centred style has been connected with promoting a child's passivity and dependency on adult control and guidance, and with low motivation for schoolwork (Aunola et al., 2000; Baumrind, 1991). Adolescents can feel controlled, devalued and criticized (Baumrind, 1991; Barber, 1996). The Indulgent-permissive and the Indifferent-uninvolved parenting patterns are found in "non-demanding" family environments. These reflect uncontrolled situations that do not encourage self-regulation in children and may leave them more impulsive (Aunola et al., 2000; Baumrind, 1991) – a condition that can be associated with underachievement at school.

We used four parenting typologies based on democratic and authoritarian styles. The Non-demanding typology (compared with two non-demanding styles above) was identified by low ratings in both democratic and autocratic styles. These parents allow autonomous, independent, immature behaviour, and show a lack of parental direction. Secondly, the Democratic typology was described by high ratings of democratic and low in authoritarian styles, and the Authoritarian typology was as well described by high ratings in authoritarian and low in democratic styles. Finally the High-demanding typology included ratings both high in democratic and authoritarian styles.

WHY SHOULD THE STYLES MATCH?

Due to similarities between behaviours of positive coaches (Chelladurai & Saleh, 1980) and democratic parents (Aunola et al., 2000; Baumrind, 1991) adolescent players can understand the meanings in communication, and feel safe with the sport. Both democratic coaches and parents listen, negotiate, and answer questions. They both allow repeated participation in decision-making, demand and support. Social Support coaches and democratic parents create warm interpersonal relations and atmosphere with acceptance and involvement. Training and Instruction coaching, and explaining, teaching democratic parenting parallel. Finally, Positive feedback /rewards giving coaching and democratic parenting show similarities. Democratic parents tell when the child has succeeded and share the good feeling. In contrast, both autocratic coaches and authoritarian parents stress personal authority and an adult monopoly in decision-making. Both use punishments before rewards (Barber, 1996; Chelladurai & Riemer, 1998; Chelladurai & Saleh, 1980). On the contrary, the Non-demanding parenting does not equate with any coaching behaviour due to the lack of parental direction, and aim-orientation, which is crucial in sport (Onatsu-Arvilommi, Nurmi & Aunola, 1998). In contrast, one aim of players in ice hockey is to work hard, learn, practice, and improve. Any positive coach, therefore, demands, gives orders, teaches and promotes the development of players (Chelladurai & Riemer, 1998). Due to differences between coaching and parenting adolescent players can find an arena in which to learn important skills, values and rules that they have not learned at home. Thus, the Positive Coaching may compensate the deficits of homes (Barnett, Smoll, & Smith, 1992).

Parents may also influence their children's expectations of coaching behaviours through their own roles as expectancy socializers, (Babkess & Weiss, 1999; Frome & Eccles, 1998). Therefore, we wanted to explore if, the interaction between Positive coaching and specific parenting typologies affects players' perceptions on cohesion, and adds to cohesion due to (1) similar matching coaching-parenting pairs, or (2) different/compensating coaching-parenting pairs. The interaction between the Autocratic coaching and parenting typologies was also examined with study.

As players get older, human-related and responsive coaching behaviour decreases (Liukkonen & Laakso & Telama, 1996; Wong & Bridges, 1995). Moreover, adolescent athletes learn from important adults other than their parents during the independent development phase of adolescence (Blos, 1979; Mazor & Enright, 1988; McGuire & Cook, 1985). Therefore, and because the dropout rates in Finland were highest with 14- and 16-year-old players (Bitti Oy, 2000), these age groups were included in our study.

METHODS

The participants were 1018 ice hockey players and their parents (n=979; mothers: n=500 and fathers: n=376; sex of parents not indicated: n=103). The sample was all 14 and 16 year-old ice-hockey players in four different ice hockey districts in Finland who were members of the Finnish Ice Hockey Association to take part (N=3233) along with their parents. This indicates a response rate of 31%.

These ages were originally chosen because of the big dropout rate after the ages of 14 and 16. At 16, players had finished the nine years of compulsory school and had to choose whether to apply to a secondary school that would lead to university, or to work.

Then we checked the proportions of forwards (39%), defenders (32%), centres (17%), and goalkeepers (12%) within our sample of 1018 respondents. The sample reflected the general pattern of players per position in ice hockey.

Players received the questionnaires at the beginning of the season. Of 1018 answers 949 players told us that they were able to play (i.e., they had access to a team). Only 36 players were considering quitting to compete in another activity, and 15 players mentioned dropping out because of the expense involved. Two players reported that they dropped out because their whole team had quit, but that they were still willing to play.

Procedure

Players were asked to answer and mail the questionnaires back to the Finnish Ice Hockey Association. Their parents were also asked to fill in a set of questionnaires dealing with their own parenting styles. Although it had been easier to ask boys to rate the caring behaviour of their parents, we did not want to take a risk with their loyalty to their parents, or to find the questionnaires too demanding. On the contrary the perceptions about coaches have been more objective and more neutral compared to coaches own ratings in many studies (Salminen & Liukkonen, 1996).

MEASUREMENTS

Coaching styles were measured using the Leadership Scale of Sport (LSS) of Chelladurai & Saleh (1980). The questionnaire comprises 40 items and the participants were asked to estimate their coaches' training practices using a 5-point Likert scale. After factor analysis (CFA, at Maximum likelihood) the dimensions, number of items, and reliabilities were: Training and Instruction (13 items, alpha .85), ("Specify in detail what is expected of each athlete."), Democratic behaviour (9 items, alpha .85), ("Let his athletes share in decision making."), Autocratic behaviour (5 items, alpha .77), ("Keep to himself."), for Social Support (8 items, (alpha .83), ("Help the athletes with their personal problems."), and Positive Feedback (5 items, alpha .82), ("Tell an athlete when he does a particularly good job."). Correlation between the "positive dimensions" varied from .37 to .57. The authors translated the questionnaire into the Finnish language for the players' sample.

Cohesion was measured by 4 questions based on the theory of cohesion (Carron, 1984; Donnelly, Carron & Chelladurai, 1979). The participants were asked to evaluate how well the following statements fit: "I really was a part of my team", "How well the members of my team got along compared with other teams", "How dependent were the players on each other", "How much did the boys help each other in games". These items were measured on a 5-point scale (1=very poor, 5=very strong). Alpha Cronbach for the measure was .67. On the basis of the small number of items (n=4) the observed low alpha was deemed acceptable (Hair, Anderson, Tatham & Black, 1998).

Parenting styles were measured using 28 items from the Finnish version of the revised Block's Child Rearing Practices Report, CRPR (Kochanska, 1990; Pulkkinen, 1996). Parents were asked to rate on a 4-point scale (1= "not like me at all" to 4= "very much like me") how well the description fitted their parental behaviour and attitudes.

A factor analysis was carried out (at Maximum likelihood) for the 28 items, with the criterion of forming three factors. The reliability data for the three factors were: (1) Democratic parenting style .83, ("My child and I have a good relationship"), (2) Authoritarian parenting style .70 ("It is important that children obey their parents"), and (3) Parental Stress dimension .74 ("I often feel that the task of upbringing is too much for me"; not reported here).

The parenting typologies were combined to one variable according to the level of discipline in homes: Non-demanding, Democratic, High-demanding, and Authoritarian typologies in that order. The Positive Coaching variable (continuing) and the Parenting (Discipline) variable were used in Linear Regression Analysis to find the effect on players' reported cohesion.

RESULTS

The results of the linear regression analysis revealed a statistically significant interaction effect between the Positive Coaching and the Discipline variable of parenting ($R^2 = .22$, $F (3,1014) = 95.96$, $p<0.001$; beta=-24, t=-2.13, p= 0.03) on cohesion. Main effects adjusted in the model. The more parent-centred control and discipline were rated by parents, the lower cohesion was reported in ice hockey if adolescent players experienced Positive Coaching. In other words, the more freedom these players experienced at home, the higher they rated cohesion with the Positive Coaching. The interaction effect between the Autocratic Coaching and the Discipline variable of parenting on cohesion was not significant by the linear regression analysis.

We performed two-way ANOVAs to show the form of the plots, and used the median split of the Positive Coaching with both age groups. The results (14 year-olds, in Table 1) revealed further that if the coaching was not positive, then players with the Non-demanding typology rated cohesion lowest. Thus, the different parenting/coaching combination predicted high cohesion, but only if the coach was perceived as high in Positive Coaching.

Table 1. Means (M) and standard deviations (S.D.) of cohesion for parents' self reports, and for coaching behaviour rated by 14-year-olds (N=650)

Parenting typologies N of players		Coaching behaviour					
		Positive/ 14 year-olds				Autocratic	
		High	N	Low	N	High	N
Non-demanding	M	16.06	96	14.22	96	14.78	88
192	S.D.	1.79		2.24		2.08	
Democratic	M	16.10	96	14.39	66	15.02	81
162	S.D.	1.89		1.95		2.04	
High-demanding	M	15.91	132	14.46	57	15.13	85
189	S.D.	2.38		1.99		2.45	
Authoritarian	M	15.77	66	14.66	41	15.24	51
107	S.D.	1.85		1.81		1.96	

Table 1 also presents the means of players' ratings for cohesion with the Autocratic Coaching. The 14-year-old boys from non-demanding homes rated their team's cohesion lowest, and players from authoritarian homes rated cohesion highest compared to other groups. The similarity between the Autocratic Coaching and the Authoritarian Parenting appears to have an affect on ratings of higher cohesion.

The effect of age was studied. All 16-year-old players showed high cohesion with the Positive Coaching (Table 2) in spite of parenting typologies at home. The Players from democratic and authoritarian homes rated highest. Further, in this age group, players from both high-demanding, and non-demanding homes rated cohesion lowest, especially if the coach was perceived as autocratic.

Table 2. Means (M) and standard deviations (S.D.) of cohesion for parents' self-reports, and for coaching rated by 16-year-olds (N=368)

Parenting typologies N of players		Coaching behaviour					
		Positive/ 16 year-olds				Autocratic	
		High	N	Low	N	High	N
Non-demanding	M	16.37	55	14.45	61	14.87	64
116	S.D.	2.04		2.09		2.28	
Democratic	M	16.85	41	14.91	43	15.13	32
84	S.D.	1.73		2.16		2.21	
High-demanding	M	16.52	33	14.43	50	14.59	48
83	S.D.	1.87		2.13		2.24	
Authoritarian	M	16.54	44	15.04	41	15.44	46
85	S.D.	1.81		2.20		2.17	

DISCUSSION

The purpose of the study was, to explore (1) the interaction effect between similar behaviour patterns from home and sport on players' reported cohesion, and (2) the effect of interaction between different and probably compensating behaviour patterns on cohesion. Moreover, we wanted to study the effect of age to adolescent players' reactions to coaching and cohesion.

The results suggest that adolescent players tended to reflect the similarity in leadership behaviours between home and sport from both democratic and authoritarian background. The similarity of meanings helps players to express ideas, understand demands and mutual responses in relations. In this study, the quality of social support, democratic leading, teaching individually, and giving rewards when they are deserved, shows the importance of those meanings. With the authoritarian parenting reflecting an autocratic approach, a player who is not used to express his own ideas at home can find the positive, democratically teaching coaching to be too demanding or stressful, and thus this has a negative effect. Instead, the similarity between adult-centred, non-responding but demanding parents and coaches appears to add cohesion compared to other players' ratings. In most studies an autocratic style has been associated with low cohesion (Hastie, 1995; Weiss & Friedrichs, 1986), which is confirmed by our data with other players.

Our results also revealed that the Positive Coaching is critical for boys from non-demanding homes in both age groups. For them a good coach demands involvement among players and encourages their development by teaching, negotiating, and supporting their positive social relations in a team. Some players do not experience this kind of support from their parents, and therefore participation in sport with a good coach can compensate the positive experiences missing in their homes. Moreover, when parents deploy low authoritarian dimensions in their caring style (i.e. when punishments are not used in their homes) then these players are more motivated by the acceptance shown by their coach, yet they showed very low cohesion if they received punishments rather than encouragement.

According to the theory of important other adults (Blos, 1979; Mazor & Enright, 1988; McGuire & Cook, 1985) and our findings, the players accepted the difference between styles of adults better at the age of 16 than 14 if the coaching behaviour was more positive than parenting at home (Authoritarian, Non-demanding). However, those from non-demanding or high-demanding homes perceived cohesion lowest when the Autocratic Coaching increased and the Positive Coaching decreased. The independency development appears to make a difference between adolescents from different kinds of homes on sport.

Yet, there are some limitations to the study. First, we had only male players in the study. Secondly, although we got many responses (1018) the willingness to answer us has probably been better if we had sent our questionnaires at the end of the season, instead of the beginning of the next, because many ice hockey teams had broken up for the summer.

CONCLUSION

The amount of authoritarian parents compared to democratic or non-demanding parents were low. If the democratic or non-demanding parenting styles increase in our society, the style of teaching and coaching must reflect this reality. Future research should take into consideration the changing needs of families, girls and boys - in both sport and schools.

This research suggests a new area of work that needs development. Non-demanding and authoritarian parenting styles have been shown to be associated with children's low motivation, and task-irrelevant achievement strategies at school (Aunola et al., 2000; Barber, 1996; Baumrind, 1991). Our study confirms the findings in ice hockey in Finland, but only if, the important adult who leads the team is experienced as non-positive or strictly autocratic. The experience of a good co-operating team is due to the democratic teaching and supporting adult in charge. Thus, adult leaders and teachers have a responsibility to add to the co-operation and trust in the team, and to help individual adolescent players to feel better, more motivated and more self-confident (as Barnett et al., 1992 suggest). Compared to schools, coaches spend far more time with adolescents in a sporting environment, and they may teach more individually.

This study has some serious implications for sport policy makers, coaches and parents, and it is clear that further research is needed to this area to ensure that we can create a supportive and responsive environment for adolescent's in sport.

REFERENCES

Aunola, K., Stattin, H., & Nurmi, J. - E. (2000). Parenting styles and adolescents' achievement strategies. *Journal of Adolescence, 23*, 205 -222.

Babkes, M.L., & Weiss, M. (1999). Parental Influence on Children's Cognitive and Affective Responses to Competitive Soccer Participation, *Pediatric Exercise Science, 11*, 44-62.

Barber, B. K. (1996). Parental psychological control: Revisiting a neglected construct. *Child Development, 67*, 3296 - 3319.

Barnett, N. P., Smoll, F. L., & Smith, R. E. (1992). Effects of enhancing coach-athlete relationships on youth sport attrition. *Sport Psychologist, 6*, 111 -127.

Baumrind, D. (1991). The influence of parenting style on adolescent competence and substance use. *Journal of Early Adolescence, 11*, 56 - 95.

Blos, P. (1979). The second individuation process of adolescence. in A. Esman. (Ed.) *The Psychology of Adolescence. Essential Readings*. NY: International University Press.

Carron, A. V. (1984). Cohesion in Sport Teams. In J. M. Silva, & R.S. Weinberg (Eds.), *Psychological Foundations of Sport*. USA: Human Kinetics.

Carron, A, V., & Hausenblas, H.A. (1998). Group dynamics in sport (2nd ed.) Morgantown, WV: Fitness Information Technology.

Chelladurai, P. (1981). The coach as motivator and chameleon of leadership styles. Science Periodical on Research and Technology in Sport. Ottawa: Coaching Association of Canada.

Chelladurai, P., & Saleh, S. (1980). Dimensions of leader behavior in sports; Development of a leadership scale. *Journal of Sport Psychology, 2*, 34-45.

Chelladurai, P., & Riemer. H. A. (1998). Measurement of leadership in sport. In J. L. Duda (Ed.), *Advances in sport and exercise psychology measurement* (pp. 227-257). Morgantown, WV: Fitness Information Technology.

Dobosz, R. P., & Beaty, L. A. (1999). The relationship between athletic participation and high school student's leadership ability. *Adolescence, 34*, 215-220.

Donnelly, P., Carron, A., & Chelladurai, P. (1979). Group cohesion and sport. *Cahper: Sociology of Sport Monograph Series*, Ottava, Canada.

Frome, P.M., & Eccles, J.S. (1998). Parents' influence on children's achievement-related perceptions. *Journal of Personality and Social Psychology, 74*, 435-452.

Gardner, D., Shields, D., Bredemeier, B., & Bostrom, A. (1996). The relationship between perceived coaching behaviors and team cohesion among baseball and softball players. *Sport Psychologist, 10*, 367- 381.

Hair, J. F., Anderson, R. F., Tatham, R. L., & Black, W.C. (1998). Multivariate data analysis. (5th ed.) New Jersey: Prentice Hall.

Hastie, P. A. (1995). Factors affecting coaching preferences of secondary school volleyball players. *Perceptual and motor skills, 80*, 347-350.

Kochanska, G. (1990). Maternal beliefs as long-term predictors of mother-child interaction and report. *Child Development, 61*, 1934-1943.

Liukkonen, J., Laakso, L., & Telama, R. (1996). Educational perspectives of youth sport coaches: Analysis of observed coaching behaviors. *International Journal of Sport Psychology. 27*, 439 -453.

Maccoby, E. E., & Martin, J.A. (1983). Socialization in the context of family: Parent-child interaction. In P.H. Mussen, & E. M. Hetherington, (Eds.), *Handbook of child psychology: Vol. 4*, Socialization, personality, and social development (4th. ed.), New York: Wiley.

Mazor, A., & Enright, R.D. (1988). The development of the individuation process from a social cognitive perspective. *Journal of Adolescence, 11*, 29-47.

McGuire, R. T., & Cook, D.L. (1985). The influence of others and the decision to participate in youth sports. *Journal of Sport Behavior, 6*, 9-16.

Muchinsky, P.M. (2003). Psychology applied to work. Belmont, CA: Thomson-Wadsworth.

Onatsu-Arvilommi, T. P., Nurmi, J. – E., & Aunola, K. (1998). Mothers' and Fathers' well-being, parenting styles, and their children's cognitive and behavioural strategies at primary school. *European Journal of Psychology of Education, 13*, 543 - 556.

Pulkkinen, L. (1996). *Kasvatuslomake.* (Parent Rearing Style questionnaire.) University of Jyväskylä, Finland.

Salminen, S., & Liukkonen, J. (1996). Coach-athlete relationship and coaching behavior in training sessions. *International Journal of Sport Psychology*, 27, 59-67.

Salokun, S. (1990). Comparison of Nigerian high school male athletes and nonathletes on self concept. *Perceptual and Motor Skills, 70*, 865 - 866.

Schliesman, E. (1987). Relationship between the congruence of preferred and actual leader behavior and subordinate satisfaction with leadership. *Journal of Sport Behavior, 10*, 157-166.

Weiss, M. R., & Friedrichs, W. D. (1986). The influence of leader behaviours, coach attributes, and institutional variables on performance and satisfaction of collegiate basketball teams. *Journal of Sport Psychology, 8*, 332 - 346.

Westre, K. R., & Weiss, M. (1991). The relationship between perceived coaching behaviors and group cohesion in high school football teams. *The Sport Psychologist, 5,* 41-54.

White, R., & Lippitt, R. (1968). Leader behavior and member reaction in three "social climates. "In D. Cartwright, & A. Zander (Eds.), *Group dynamics: Research and theory* (pp. 318-335). NY: Harper & Row.

Wong, E., & Bridges, L. (1995). Age-related differences in inter- and intrapersonal variables related to motivation in a group sport setting. *Current Directions in Psychological Science, 6,* 16 -21.

In: Motivation of Exercise and Physical Activity
Editor: Liam A. Chiang, pp. 105-117

ISBN: 978-1-60021-596-4
© 2007 Nova Science Publishers, Inc.

Chapter 8

FOSTERING EXERCISE MOTIVATION AND PROMOTING PHYSICAL ACTIVITY THROUGH A PHYSICAL EDUCATION PEDOMETER PROGRAM

Paul M. Wright[*], *Weidong Li, Diane Coleman and Ben Dyson*
The University of Memphis, Tennessee, USA

ABSTRACT

Physical education is a critical site for addressing the twin epidemic of obesity and physical inactivity. It has been suggested that combining pedometer use with goal setting may be an effective way to foster exercise motivation and promote physical activity. To date, research on this topic has focused on high school students and adults. The current study used a program evaluation framework and mixed methods to explore the feasibility of an upper elementary physical education pedometer program. Participants were 217 3rd (54), 4th (67), 5th (51), and 6th (45) grade boys and girls. Qualitative and quantitative findings support the notion that goal-based pedometer programs can be effectively implemented in the upper elementary grades. The effectiveness of the program did not appear to be mediated by gender or grade level. It is recommended that programs of this type be introduced to pre-adolescent populations through school-based physical education to address growing rates of physical inactivity and obesity. Future studies should explore the impact of such programs on the actual activity levels, relevant psychological constructs, and future health status of participants.

[*] Please send all correspondence to: Paul M. Wright, Ph.D.; Department of Health and Sport Sciences, University of Memphis, Memphis, TN; (901) 678-3480; pwright2@memphis.edu

INTRODUCTION

Obesity has taken on an epidemic proportion in recent years. According to the Centers for Disease Control & Prevention (CDC), obesity-related illness will soon become the leading cause of death in the USA (CDC, 2004). While the etiology of obesity is complex, physical activity plays a fundamental role in body weight and obesity status. There is strong evidence showing that physical activity levels among children and youth have decreased dramatically in recent years (United States Department of Health & Human Services (USDHHS), 2001), and the most pronounced drop in physical activity occurs during adolescence (Adams, Schoenborn, Moss, Warren & Kahn, 1995; Grunbaum, et al., 2004; Kulinna, Martin, Lai, Kilber & Reed, 2003). Therefore, fostering exercise motivation and promoting physical activity prior to adolescence has become a public health priority to win the battle against obesity (CDC, 1997, 2001; USDHHS, 2000, 2001).

In a special report by the Surgeon General, schools were identified as the most logical setting to foster exercise motivation and promote physical activity (USDHHS, 2001). It has been argued that school-based physical education in particular should prepare students for life-long physical activity (CDC, 1997; USDHHS, 2000). The National Association of Sport and Physical Education (NASPE) states that a physically educated person must be fit, be skilled, know the benefits of physical activity, and value physical activity (NASPE, 1995, 2004). Since most youth have nine years of required physical education in school, this institution is positioned to have a meaningful impact (Sallis & McKenzie, 1991; McKenzie, 2003). When implemented effectively, research has demonstrated that school-based physical education can increase physical activity levels and improve physical fitness (Kahn, et al., 2002), as well as reduce levels of overweight among students (Datar & Sturm, 2004).

To promote lifelong physical activity and fitness, Corbin (2002) proposes physical education programs should: (a) recognize the unique physical activity needs of youth, (b) promote opportunities for all students to be physically active (c) promote self-esteem and feelings of confidence, and (e) emphasize self-management skills to enhance lifelong participation in physical activity. A growing body of practice-based literature suggests that combining pedometer use with goal setting may be an effective way to motivate students and teach self-management skills. The integration of pedometers and goal setting strategies (Butler & Anderson, 2002; Hutchinson & Mercier, 2004; Martinez, 2004) in physical education is increasingly embraced by practitioners. Through monitoring daily activity levels, providing immediate feedback on activity levels, and being an exercise reminder, pedometers can be used as a motivational tool for exercise (Brewer & Nelson, 2005; Cagle, 2004; Dunn & Tannehill, 2005; Ladda, Keating, Adams, & Toscano, 2004). Goal setting can be used to sustain and increase students' engagement and motivation (Anderson, 2002). Specifically, goal setting assists students by directing their attention to a specific target, mobilizing their effort relative to the task demands, and providing a reference point to evaluate their performance as well as a reason to persist in the activity over time (Locke & Latham, 1990).

The most convincing evidence to date regarding the impact of pedometer interventions has focused on adult populations. In a preliminary study on the impact of a pedometer-based intervention with an adult population, Croteau (2004) demonstrated an increase in self-reported daily steps as well as more positive perceptions of physical activity. Over the course of an eight-week program, the average steps per day increased from 8,565 to 10,538 for the

37 participants. Obese and overweight participants increased their number of steps by 34.3% and 24%, respectively. Across the entire sample, mean scores related to perceptions of physical activity increased from neutral to moderately positive. Glazener et al. (2004) also reported increases in physical activity as measured by pedometers in an adult female population. Using a quasi-experimental design, it was demonstrated that participants who were given specific targets and structured goals significantly increased their number of daily steps as compared to participants in a control condition who were not provided with specific targets or goal setting strategies. The steady increase in the average number of daily steps among treatment participants resulted in a clear linear trend that was not seen among control participants. A similar study was carried out with 165 high school physical education students (Zizzi et al., 2006). In this study, there were no significant changes in either group: pedometer only or pedometer plus goal setting. The failure to find significant impact may be due to the short (three weeks) intervention period.

In light of the practical support and related empirical literature, the purpose of the current study was to explore the feasibility of a pedometer program delivered in an upper-elementary physical education program. Because there is a "drop off" in physical activity as students grow older, it is important to identify interventions that can be delivered prior to adolescence. Since the decrease in activity is more prevalent in girls than boys (Kulinna, et al., 2003; McKenzie, 2001, 2003), it also is important to identify interventions that do not appear to have a gender bias. Based on this rationale, the purpose of the current study was to explore 3rd-6th grade students' perceptions of a goal-based pedometer program, and investigate gender and grade differences in motivation in the pedometer program. A program evaluation framework using mixed methods was employed (Onwuegbuzie & Teddlie, 2003). Guiding evaluation questions included: 1) Was the program delivered effectively?; 2) Was the program received and understood by participants?; and 3) How did participants perceive the program?

METHOD

Participants and Setting

Participants were 217 3rd (54), 4th (67), 5th (51), and 6th (45) graders enrolled in a co-educational physical education. Each grade level was represented by more than one class section, with a total of seven class sections involved. Of the total sample there were 106 boys (48.8%) and 111 girls (51.2%). This study was conducted in the southern region of the USA where rates of obesity, childhood obesity, and obesity-related diseases are the highest (CDC, 2004; Grunbaum et al., 2004). All classes were taught twice per week by an experienced, certified physical education teacher at a University campus school. Parental consent was secured for all participants and the study was approved by the university's Institutional Review Board and the school's principal.

Procedure

To ensure that all classes received the same information and training, the physical education teacher followed specific lesson plans in the pedometer program. In the 5-week program, participants were taught how and why to use pedometers (Cagle, 2004; Dunn & Tannehill, 2005). Specifically, the basic function of pedometers was explained as well as the benefits of wearing them and the recommended number of daily steps for health promotion. The introductory lessons also addressed the correct use and care of the pedometers (Brewer & Nelson, 2005). After introductory lessons that included practice using pedometers, participants began a daily routine of documenting the number of steps taken during the physical education class. The physical education teacher helped participants record their number of steps at the end of each lesson. After a full week of data was collected as a baseline for comparison, participants were introduced to the concept and process of goal setting (Locke & Latham, 1990). The lessons on goal setting included defining goals, providing examples of goals in varied settings, and emphasizing the key components of a SMART (Specific, Measurable, Attainable, Realistic, and Timely) goal. Varied pedagogical strategies, such as direct instruction, checks for understanding, and group discussion were incorporated in all pedometer lessons.

The physical education teacher guided participants through the process of setting challenging goals, recording progress daily, and adjusting goals as needed in each subsequent week. It was made clear to participants that the objective of this program was self-improvement and not competition. Seven classroom teachers were encouraged to deliver reinforcing messages about physical activity and pedometer use during recess. A pedometer record sheet (see Figure 1) was used to document participant goals and actual performance. Weekly goals were based on the number of steps taken in physical education, but the pedometer record sheet did include space for recording steps taken during recess as well.

Data Collection

After completing the program, participants responded to five evaluation items with a 6-point likert scale. Individual items were used to assess participants' intention to use pedometers after school, the importance of doing well in the program, and their perceived effort in the program. Two items were used to assess participants' interest. As the internal consistency Cronbach Coefficient alpha (Cronbach, 1951) for the two interest items was 0.92, their average value was used for data analysis. Participants also completed four open response items. Three of these assessed their comprehension of the material covered. These items included "What did you learn from the pedometer program?"; "Why should people wear pedometers?"; and "Describe any problems that you had with setting goals." The final item provided participants the opportunity to add any additional comments. Additional data sources included video-taping of selected lessons, non-participant observations, informal interviews with the physical education teacher, as well as post-program evaluations completed by the classroom teachers. Classroom teacher evaluation items included: "Did you hear any comments about the program from students?"; "What are your perceptions of the pedometer program?"; "Did wearing pedometers have any impact on your students' activity and/or participation levels?"; "What differences, if any, do you see in your students before and after wearing the pedometers?"; and "Please identify students who have become more active after the pedometer program."

PEDOMETER RECORD SHEET

*Student Name*_____

*Teacher*_____

*Grade*_____

Date	Number of Steps In Physical Education	Goal for Steps in Physical Education Next Week	Did you make it? (Yes or No)	Number of steps During Recess				
				Mon	Tue	Wed	Thur	Fri

Figure 1. Pedometer Record Sheet.

Data Analysis

Correlational analysis was used to examine relationships among participants' intention to use pedometers after school, the importance of doing well in the program, perceived effort, and interest. A two-way nonparametric MANOVA was used to investigate whether participants' perceptions were a function of gender and grade level.

Qualitative data were analyzed inductively to identify meaningful patterns (Patton, 2002). Transcripts from selected lessons were analyzed using a rubric to assess the fidelity of implementation. For each key point from a given lesson, researchers assigned one of three ratings: 1) addressed the point directly as planned; 2) addressed the point indirectly or partially; and 3) did not address the point. All qualitative data were analyzed by at least two members of the research team. Researcher and data triangulation as well as peer debriefing strategies were used to establish trustworthiness (Lincoln & Guba, 1985). Complete consensus was reached on all qualitative patterns and ratings before analysis was considered final.

RESULTS

Was the Program Delivered Effectively?

The physical education teacher delivered lessons on pedometer use and goal setting with a high degree of fidelity. Two members of the research team reviewed the video-taped sessions and confirmed that all key points from the lesson plans were addressed. Using a predetermined rubric the reviewers were in 100% agreement in their ratings. When introducing pedometers, the physical education teacher clearly explained their function and the reason people wear them. She asked many probing questions to check for understanding and allowed multiple students the opportunity to respond. She also explained that the recommended number of daily steps for health promotion is 10,000. After providing instruction on pedometer use and letting students practice with them, the physical education teacher emphasized that the pedometer program was about individual improvement and not competition. In one class she stated, "We're not having a competition between people in the class to see if you have the most steps. Your competition is with yourself, so that you can see if you can take more steps." In another class she said, "The numbers don't mean anything to anybody else but you. There's not a competition to see who's got the highest number. Your competition is with yourself. OK?"

When she introduced goal setting, the physical education teacher began by defining goals and giving examples of goals in varied settings. She allowed students to offer their own examples to check for understanding and clarify any confusion. Due to the structure of the program, all goals were specific, measurable, and timely. Therefore, instruction on these aspects of SMART goals was sometimes indirect. However, the physical education teacher directly addressed the importance of making goals attainable and realistic. She conveyed this message in statements such as, "You don't want to make it too high so that you can't make it", and "It's OK if you set a goal that you find out is kind of easy, because next week you can set another one that might be more".

While the primary focus of the program was the physical education setting, participants' classroom teachers (N=7) were asked to send reinforcing messages and encourage participants to use pedometers during recess. In open responses to a post-program evaluation, these teachers shared their perspective. Teachers generally believed that the program was a positive and engaging experience for students. Teachers stated, "Students were excited about wearing them", "Students talked of competition about who would have the highest score", and "They would compete with each other or else set personal best goals." All teachers supported the use of pedometers. Positive comments included, "I think it is good for the students to wear pedometers in order to encourage them to be more active", and "Good, - it motivated them to be more active during recess." The majority of teachers believed that students were more active when wearing the pedometer. One teacher stated that the pedometers had a "bigger impact of awareness" on the students. Others commented students were "More aware of how much they walk, run, etc.", and "I saw them being more active at recess." However, teachers were less sure that they had seen differences in the students before and after the pedometer program. Five of the seven teachers were able to identify at least one student who they believed became more active as a result of the program. One of these teachers felt that here entire class had become more active during recess.

Daily records of participant steps and written goals provided strong evidence that the program was delivered with a high degree of consistency and fidelity. While there did not appear to be any difference in the way the intervention was delivered or received, the physical education teacher noted the 5th grade students involved in this study were more challenging than usual. This was not attributed to or observed only in the pedometer program. In sum, multiple data sources indicated that program fidelity was high and consistent across the four grade levels.

Was the Program Received and Understood by Participants?

As noted above, key points of instruction were delivered consistently in all class sections but the examples used and the flow of discussion varied based on participant responses and situational needs. Generally, the participants appeared engaged and receptive. The physical education teacher and trained observers both noted that participants were quite curious and somewhat distracted by the pedometers early in the program. Some students would hop up and down, run in place, or shake the pedometer to increase the count. At one point the physical education teacher explained, "Standing and shaking your pedometer or jumping up and down means you don't reach your goal. It's got to be activities you do in PE that help you reach your goal." Despite the fact that the physical education teacher discouraged students from competing with one another, some students frequently checked their count and compared it with their peers'. This was also observed by the classroom teachers at recess. However, these behaviors seemed to decrease with each passing week in the physical education setting as pedometer use became routine.

Qualitative analysis of participants' open responses indicated that the main lessons of the program were understood. When asked "What did you learn from the pedometer program?", participants from each grade level demonstrated a reasonable amount of understanding. Simplistic responses to this item included, "I learned how many steps I take", "how to use a pedometer", "I learned that taking steps is fun", and "I learned it doesn't matter who takes the most steps." Participants from grades 5 and 6 often conveyed a higher level of comprehension, i.e. "We need to take many steps to stay healthy", "The pedometer tells you how many calories you lost", "I need to walk and exercise daily to lose weight and stay in shape and lower my calories", and "It is important to take steps than just watching T.V. It's real good for your health."

In response to the item "Why should people wear pedometers?", participants again displayed a reasonable level of comprehension. Even 3rd and 4th graders offered accurate information such as "To monitor your exercise", "To see how many calories you burn", "To set goals for yourself", and "To be healthy." Again, 5th and 6th graders demonstrated a higher degree of cognitive ability and writing skill. For instance, these older participants made the following statements, "So you can stay healthy by trying to take more steps a day", and "You can lose weight from how many steps you take." It was noted that several students had a misperception that pedometers were valuable because they could determine "how much weight you lost."

When asked to "Describe any problems that you had with setting goals", some 3rd and 4th graders indicated that they struggled with the goal setting process and some were confused about the potential benefits of wearing a pedometer; a fourth grade participant asked: "How do you lose weight with a pedometer?" One 5th grader stated, "That reaching your goal is harder than I thought." Additional comments offered by participants were generally positive. These included, "I like the pedometer program because we can't do anything wrong", "I wish we could do more with the pedometers", "I would prefer that our school should wear them more often", and "Pedometers rock!"

How did Participants Perceive the Program?

Participants reported positive ratings (six being the most positive) on all quantitative variables: intention to use pedometers after school (M=4.8, SD=1.62), interest (M=4.66, SD=1.41), importance of doing well (M=4.53, SD=1.45), and effort (M=5.1, SD=1.25). Correlational analysis indicated mutually positive relationships between the four variables with coefficients ranging from 0.44 to 0.67. Interest in the pedometer program was linked to higher levels of importance and effort and intention to use pedometers after school. These descriptive statistics and correlation coefficients are displayed in Table 1. Table 2 and Table 3 display means and standard deviations for grade level and gender, respectively.

Table 1. Means, Standard Deviations, and Correlation Coefficients for all Variables (N=214)

Variable	M	SD	1	2	3	4
1. Intention to use pedometers after school	4.80	1.62	--	.67*	.50*	.44*
2. Interest	4.66	1.41		--	.56*	.65*
3. Importance of doing well	4.53	1.45			--	.53*
4. Effort	5.10	1.25				--

Table 2. Means and Standard Deviations for all Variables by Grade Levels

Variable	Grade 3		Grade 4		Grade 5		Grade 6	
	M	SD	M	SD	M	SD	M	SD
Intention to use pedometers after school	5.04	1.62	4.57	1.77	4.42	1.70	5.29	1.06
Interest	4.91	1.30	4.65	1.52	4.12	1.57	5.00	0.98
Importance of doing well	4.79	1.47	4.62	1.43	4.12	1.60	4.56	1.22
Effort	5.15	1.35	5.30	1.03	4.58	1.50	5.36	0.93

Table 3. Means and Standard Deviations for all Variables by Gender

Variable	*Male*		Female	
	M	SD	M	SD
Intention to use pedometers after school	4.63	1.66	4.96	1.57
Interest	4.54	1.49	4.77	1.33
Importance of doing well	4.22	1.47	4.81	1.38
Effort	5.00	1.39	5.20	1.11

The MANOVA and follow-up ANOVAs indicated idiosyncratic grade differences in participants' perceptions, $F(12, 526.8)=2.27$, $p<0.0082$. However, perceptions were not a function of gender and the interaction of gender and grade. Follow-up ANOVAs showed significant grade differences in intention to use pedometers after school ($F(3, 202)=5.17$, $p<0.0018$), interest ($F(3, 202)=4.75$, $p<0.0032$), and effort ($F(3, 202)=4.56$, $p<0.0041$. Participants at Grade 3 ($p<0.0009$, ES=0.37) and Grade 6 ($p<0.0011$, ES=0.61) reported higher levels of intention to use pedometers after school as compared to those at Grade 5. Participants at Grade 3 ($p<0.0017$, ES=0.55), Grade 4 ($p<0.0056$, ES=0.34), and Grade 6 ($p<0.0013$, ES=0.66) reported higher levels of interest in the pedometer program as compared to those at Grade 5. Participants at Grade 3 ($p<0.0029$, ES=0.40), Grade 4 ($p<0.0021$, ES=0.57), and Grade 6 ($p<0.0029$, ES=0.62) reported higher levels of effort in the pedometer program as compared to those at Grade 5.

CONCLUSION

The purpose of the current study was to explore the feasibility of delivering a goal-based pedometer program in upper-elementary physical education. While a growing body of literature indicates that goal-based pedometer programs can be effective in promoting physical activity, these studies have involved adult or teen-age participants (Croteau, 2004; Glazener, et al., 2004; Zizzi, et al., 2006). However, the trend toward decreased physical activity is most pronounced in the adolescent years (Adams, et al., 1995; Grunbaum, et al., 2004; Kulinna, et al., 2003). It stands to reason, therefore, that programs designed to prevent this decline and the related increase in obesity should target pre-adolescents. The results of the current study demonstrate that elementary students as young as 3rd graders can fully participate in, comprehend, and enjoy a pedometer program.

Due to the exploratory nature of this study, it was important to examine potential differences related to grade-level and gender. While there were no systematic grade differences in participant perceptions, the level of cognitive understanding related to the benefits of pedometers and the goal setting process appear higher among 5th and 6th graders in comparison to 3rd and 4th graders. Although females are often less physically active and less motivated in physical education than males (Kulinna, et al., 2003; McKenzie, 2001, 2003), the current study demonstrated that both genders were equally engaged in the pedometer program.

It is suggested that physical education teachers integrate activities into their curriculum to promote exercise motivation and physical activity (CDC, 1997; USDHHS, 2000). This is largely in response to the public health crisis related to physical inactivity and obesity (CDC, 2004; USDHHS, 2001). While actual physical activity levels are not reported here, formative data suggest that pedometer programs have the potential to influence students' activity levels inside and outside the school setting. Current findings indicate that a goal-based pedometer program can elicit positive ratings of motivational responses such as interest and perceived effort, as well as perceived importance of the program and participants' intention to use pedometers outside of school. Based on this, the intermediate impact on physical activity levels and relevant constructs such as intrinsic motivation should be explored in future studies. The ultimate endpoint in this line of research would be the prevention of obesity and obesity related illness. To study impact at this level would require randomized clinical trials with sufficient follow-up periods.

The results of this study indicate that upper elementary students are fully capable of learning to use pedometers and setting goals related to their physical activity levels. Self-monitoring skills and behaviors of this type should be integrated in physical education if we truly want to promote lifelong physical activity (Corbin, 2002). Moreover, these skills, behaviors, and dispositions need to be introduced before it is too late, i.e. before students have already begun losing their interest and motivation for exercise and physical activity. It is suggested, therefore, that practitioners consider integrating programs of this type into the physical education curriculum as early as possible. While most physical education teachers will not be in a position to know the ultimate impact on their students' future health status, in the short term they can be assured that program of this type are aligned with the national standards for physical education (NASPE, 2004) and represents current educational best practice by incorporating authentic learner assessment (NASPE, 1995), integrating technology (Ladda, et al., 2004), and actively engaging students (Anderson, 2002).

While the program studied here was successful, the degree to which these results can be generalized requires some discussion. This study was conducted in a large urban school district in the Southern USA with extremely high rates of obesity and physical inactivity. Demonstrating feasibility in this environment is meaningful based on the relevance of the problem to the local population. Although only one school was involved, seven different class sections and 217 individual students participated. This research design would not be sufficient for making causal inferences, but is more than adequate for a feasibility study using a program evaluation framework. The most noteworthy issue limiting generalization has to do with the school's university affiliation. Although this school is part of an urban district, its connection to the university has a clear, positive impact on school culture. The willingness of the physical education teacher and classroom teachers to deliver the program required an engaged and collaborative faculty as well as a supportive administration. Because action research projects are common in this school, students are also more familiar with and receptive to such activities. While these factors facilitated implementation in the current study, reproducing these results in other school environments may be more challenging. Specific obstacles may include: a) physical education teachers who are less qualified and effective; b) classroom teachers who are not as willing to collaborate; c) administrators who assign lower status and less support to physical education; and d) student and parent populations who are less open to innovation, especially as it relates to the traditional roles and activities associated with physical education. Problems of this type are common in physical education, especially in urban environments (Ennis, 1999) and could limit the effectiveness of this program or any other.

In sum, the results of the current study support the notion that goal-based pedometer programs can be effectively implemented in the upper elementary grades. It is recommended that programs of this type be introduced to pre-adolescent populations through school-based physical education to address growing rates of physical inactivity and obesity in our nation (Corbin, 2002). Future studies should explore the impact of such programs on the actual activity levels, relevant psychological constructs, and future health status of participants. Practitioners may implement programs of this type for their educational value, although the fidelity of implementation may be mediated by the district and school context.

REFERENCES

Adams, P., Schoenborn, C., Moss, A., Warren, C, & Kahn, L. (1995). Health-risk behaviors among our nation's youth: United States, 1992. Hyattsville, MD: U.S. Department of Health and Human Services, Public Health Service, CDC, 1995. DHHS publication no. (PHS) 95-1520. (Vital and health statistics; series 10, no. 192).

Anderson, A. (2002). Engaging Student Learning in Physical Education. *Journal of Physical Education, Recreation, and Dance, 73*, 35-39.

Brewer, J., Nelson, S. (2005). Using and Caring for Pedometers. *Strategies, 3*, 28-29.

Butler, L. F., Anderson, S. P. (2002). Inspiring Students to a Lifetime of Physical Activity. *Journal of Physical Education, Recreation, and Dance, 73*, 21-25.

Cagle, B. (2004). Stepping Up with Pedometers. *Strategies, 1*, 27-28.

CDC. (1997). Guidelines for school and community programs to promote lifelong physical activity among young people. *MMWR 1997; 46*(No. RR-6).

CDC. (2001). Increasing physical activity: A report on recommendations of the Task Force on Community Preventive Services. MMWR 2001; 50(No.RR-18).

CDC. (2004). National Center for Chronic Disease Prevention and Health Promotion, Centers for Disease Control and Prevention. Fact sheet-Actual causes of death in the United States, 2000. March 2004. Available at http://www.cdc.gov/nccdphp/factsheets.

Corbin, C. B. (2002). Physical activity for everyone: What every physical educator should know about promoting lifelong physical activity. *Journal of Teaching in Physical Education, 21*, 128-144.

Cronbach, L.J. (1951). Coefficient alpha and the internal structure of tests. *Psychometrika, 16*, 297-334.

Croteau, K.A. (2004). A Preliminary Study on the Impact of a Pedometer-based Intervention on Daily Steps. *American Journal of Health Promotion, 18*, 217-220.

Datar, A., & Sturm, R. (2004). Physical education in elementary school and body mass index: Evidence from the Early Childhood Longitudinal Study. *American Journal of Public Health, 94*, 1501-1506.

Dunn, L. & Tannehill, D. (2005). Using Pedometers to Promote Physical Activity in Secondary Education. *Strategies, 5*, 19-25.

Ennis, C.D. (1999). Communicating the value of active, healthy lifestyles to urban students. *Quest, 51*, 164-169.

Glazener, H., DeVoe, D., Nelson, T. and Gotshall, R. (2004). Changes in physical activity influenced by using a pedometer. *Journal of Human Movement Studies, 46*, 473-482.

Grunbaum, J., Kann, L, Kinchen, S., Ross, J., Hawkins, J., Lowry, R., Harris, W., McManus, T., Chyen, D., & Collins, J. (2004) Youth Risk Behavior Surveillance-United States 2003. I Surveillance Summaries, May 21, 2004. *Morbidity and Mortality Weekly Report 2004*, 53: SS-2.

Hutchinson, G.E., Mercier, R. (2004). Using Social Psychological Concepts to Help Students. *Journal of Physical Education, Recreation, and Dance, 75*, 22-26.

Kahn, E.B., Ramsey, L.T., Brownson, R.C., Heath, G.W., Howze, E.H., Powell, K.E., Stone, E.J., Rajab, M.W., Corso, P. & the Task Force on Community Preventive Services (2002) The effectiveness of interventions to increase physical activity: A systematic review. *American Journal of Preventive Medicine, 22*, 73-107.

Kulinna, H.P., Martin, J., Lai, Q., Kilber, A., Reed, B. (2003). Student physical activity patterns: grade, gender, and activity influences. *Journal of Teaching in Physical Education, 22*, 298-310.

Ladda, S., Keating, T., Adams, D., Toscano, L. (2004). Including Technology in Instructional Programs. *Journal of Physical Education, Recreation, and Dance, 74*, 12-13.

Lincoln, Y.S., & Guba, E.G. (1985). *Naturalistic Inquiry*. Beverly Hills, CA: Sage.

Locke, E.A., & Latham, G.P. (1990). *A theory of goal setting and task performance*. Englewood Cliffs, NJ: Prentice Hall.

Martinez, R. (2004). Promoting Physical Activity through Goal Setting Strategies. *Strategies, 2*, 25-26.

McKenzie, T.L. (2001). Promoting physical activity in youth: focus on middle school environments. *Quest, 53*, 326-334.

McKenzie, T.L. (2003). Health related physical education: Physical activity, fitness, and wellness. In S. Silverman and C. Ennis (Eds.), *Student Learning in Physical Education: Applying research to enhance instruction* (pp. 207-226) Champaign, IL: Human Kinetics.

National Association for Sport and Physical Education. (1995). *Moving into the future. National standards for physical education: A guide to content and assessment*. St. Louis, MO: Mosby.

National Association for Sport and Physical Education. (2004). *Moving into the future. National standards for physical education* (2nd ed.). Reston, VA: Author.

Onwuegbuzie, A., & Teddlie, C. (2003). A framework for analyzing data in mixed methods research. In A. Tashakkorie and C. Teddlie (Eds.). *Handbook of mixed methods in social and behavioral research*. (pp. 351-383). Thousand Oaks, CA: Sage Publications.

Patton, Q.M. (2002). *Qualitative research and evaluation methods (3rd ed.)*. Thousand Oaks, CA: Sage.

Sallis, J.F., & Mckenzie, T.L. (1991). Physical Education's role in public health. *Research Quarterly for Exercise and Sport, 62*, 124-137.

U.S. Department of Health and Human Services. (2000). Healthy People 2010 (conference ed., 2 vols.). Washington, DC: U.S. Department of Health and Human Services.

U.S. Department of Health and Human Services. (2001). The Surgeon General's Call to Action to prevent and decrease overweight and obesity. Rockville, Maryland: U.S. Department of Health and Human Services, Public Health Service, Office of the Surgeon General.

Zizzi, S., Vitullo, E., Rye, J.,O'Hara Tompkins, N., Abildso, C., Fisher, B., & Bartlett, M. (2006). Impact of a Three-Week Pedometer Intervention on High School Students' Daily Step Counts and Perceptions of Physical Activity. *American Journal of Health Education, 37*, 35-40.

In: Motivation of Exercise and Physical Activity
Editor: Liam A. Chiang, pp. 119-133

ISBN: 978-1-60021-596-4
© 2007 Nova Science Publishers, Inc.

Chapter 9

DISPOSITIONAL GOAL ORIENTATIONS, MOTIVATIONAL CLIMATE, AND PSYCHOBIOSOCIAL STATES IN PHYSICAL EDUCATION

Laura Bortoli and Claudio Robazza

Facoltà di Scienze dell'Educazione Motoria, Università di Chieti, Italy

ABSTRACT

The purpose of this study was to investigate the univariate and multivariate relationships among an individual's dispositional goal orientation (task/ego), classroom motivational climate (mastery/performance), and pleasant or unpleasant psychobiosocial (PBS) states (i.e., emotion, cognition, motivation, bodily reactions, movement, performance, and communication) as conceptualized within the Individual Zones of Optimal Functioning model. The participants were 1632 Italian physical education pupils (809 girls and 823 boys, aged 11-14 years) drawn from public junior high schools. The assessment included a goal orientation questionnaire, a motivational climate inventory, and pleasant and unpleasant PBS descriptors. Hierarchical multiple regression analysis showed that an individual's task orientation was directly related to pleasant PSB states and indirectly related to unpleasant PBS states. Canonical correlation analysis indicated that task-oriented students who perceived a mastery-involving climate tended to experience high levels of pleasant states and low levels of unpleasant states. Findings suggest that physical education teachers should create a motivational mastery climate, thereby promoting task involvement and a pleasant emotional experience.

Keywords: achievement goal theory, emotions, IZOF model

In recent years, motivation research in the domain of school physical education (PE) has focused on achievement goal theory (see Biddle, 2001; Chen, 2001). The theory assumes two main dispositional goals named task orientation and ego orientation, which reflect an individual's tendency to evaluate personal success and competence in different ways (Duda & Nicholls, 1992; Nicholls, 1992). Task-oriented students usually perceive ability in a self-referenced way: they tend to be interested in personal improvement, ascribe high value to effort, and consider sport ability as a product of learning. In contrast, ego-oriented students generally perceive ability as normatively referenced: they tend to be interested in demonstrating superior ability, consider sport ability as a gift, and try to outperform others or attain better achievements with less effort than others.

Research in the PE context has shown that high task-oriented students were more intrinsically motivated (Duda, 1996), enjoyed learning experiences more frequently and felt less boredom (Spray, Biddle, & Fox, 1999), identified intrinsic reasons for discipline in PE classes (Papaioannou, 1998a), and perceived the value of mastering skills, trying hard, and cooperating with others as an important function of PE classes (Walling & Duda, 1995). The achievement goal theory also examines the relationship between an individual's dispositional goal orientation and classroom motivational climate. Rather than being conceptualized as stable traits of personality, individual goal orientations are viewed as changeable cognitive schemas that influence the perception of specific environmental cues (Roberts, 2001; Treasure, 2001).

Ames (1992a) refers to the perceived motivational climate construct to describe the individual's composite view regarding the prevalent goal structure operating in a particular achievement setting. In the school and sport context, teachers' and coaches' goals are evident by how they organize task, give recognition and rewards, group pupils, and evaluate performance. Ames (1992b) used the mastery and performance labels to distinguish between task-involvement motivational climate and ego-involvement motivational climate, respectively. A mastery-involving climate places emphasis on skill mastery, effort, and social relations, whereas a performance-involving climate draws attention on social comparison, normative-based evaluation, and competition.

Research in PE has revealed the important role of a mastery climate in increasing and sustaining students' motivation (see for reviews, Biddle, 2001; Ntoumanis & Biddle, 1999). Individual's perception of a mastery climate was related to intrinsic motivation, positive attitudes toward the lesson, high perceived ability, interest in PE, satisfaction, adaptive cognitive processes, and self-determined reasons for discipline.

In the achievement goal theory, dispositional goal orientations and perceptions of motivational climate are two independent dimensions of motivation that interact to influence behavior. Initially, these two dimensions were considered separately, but more recently the importance to evaluate their combined effects and interaction on different variables has been emphasized (Duda, 2001; Roberts, 2001; Thomas & Barron, 2006). In an interactionist approach, motivational climate (situational factor) is viewed as potentially capable of altering the individual's dispositional goal orientation (personal factor), the related probabilities of adopting a certain goal of action, and the display of a particular behavioral pattern (Treasure, 2001; Weigand & Burton, 2002).

Some studies have applied the interactionist approach in the PE context. Cury et al. (1996) assessed the influence of individual and contextual factors on adolescent girls' interest in PE. Intrinsic interest resulted to be influenced more by situational climate than by dispositional goals (mastery climate positively predicted interest, whereas performance climate was inversely related to interest). Moreover, dispositional goals were strongly influenced by their corresponding climate dimension. Papaioannou (1998a) found that task orientation and perception of a task-involving (mastery) climate were significant positive predictors of self-reported discipline, whereas ego orientation and perception of an ego-involving (performance) climate were not. Theodosiou and Papaioannou (2006) analyzed the relationship between achievement goals, motivational climate, and students' metacognitive processes. Results showed that both task-orientation and perception of a mastery climate contributed in the explanation of total variance of students' metacognitive activity. In addition, there was evidence that metacognition had a mediating role between mastery climate and task orientation on one hand, and frequency of sport and exercise involvement on the other.

Standage, Duda, and Ntoumanis (2003) examined the effects of dispositional goal orientation, motivational climate, and perceived competence on the motivational styles proposed by self-determination theory. Perceived competence, task orientation, and perceived mastery climate were positive predictors of intrinsic motivation and identified regulation, whereas ego orientation was a negative predictor of identified regulation. Significant interactions emerged for task orientation and mastery climate, and for ego orientation and perceived competence related to intrinsic motivation to know and intrinsic motivation to experience stimulation. Interaction between task orientation and mastery climate also predicted intrinsic motivation toward accomplishments. A three-way interaction between ego orientation, performance climate and perceived competence was significant in predicting intrinsic motivation to experience stimulation. The authors underlined the importance of adopting an interactionist approach for a better understanding of motivational processes in PE.

The purpose of the present study in the PE context was to investigate the univariate and multivariate relationships among individual's dispositional goal orientation (task/ego), classroom motivational climate (mastery/performance), pleasant and unpleasant emotional states and other psychobiosocial (PSB) states as conceptualized within the Individual Zones of Optimal Functioning (IZOF) model. The model has been developed by Hanin (1978, 1986) to examine the anxiety-performance relationship in the sporting domain. More recently, the model has been broadened to incorporate, in a holistic approach, a vast array of idiosyncratic emotions and additional performance-related PSB states in which the emotional experience is conceived as a crucial component (Hanin, 1997, 2000, 2004; for reviews, see Robazza, 2006; Hanin, in press). PSB states are defined as situational, multimodal, and dynamic manifestations of the total human functioning, and are described in terms of the five interrelated dimensions of form, content, intensity, context, and time. The form dimension includes seven interactive components defined as: (a) cognitive, emotional, and motivational states (psychological aspects); (b) bodily and kinesthetic states (biological aspects); (c) performance and communicative states (social aspects).

Results of the studies in which dispositional goal orientation and perceived motivational climate have been examined showed the beneficial effects of individual's task orientation and perception of a mastery climate on variables such as intrinsic motivation, reasons to be disciplined, and enjoyment for physical activity. In contrast, individual's ego orientation and perception of a performance climate were found to exert detrimental effects because related to low motivation, boredom, and anxiety. Based on these findings, we wanted to examine the single and combined effects of dispositional orientation and perceived motivational climate on PBS states as conceptualized within the IZOF model. The IZOF view was adopted as a framework for this investigation, because it provides a broad and fined-grained conceptualization of emotional states related to performance. Dispositional task orientation and mastery-involving climate were predicted to be positively related to pleasant PBS states. Conversely, ego orientation and performance-involving climate were expected to be associated with unpleasant PBS states.

METHOD

Participants

Participants were 1632 PE pupils, 809 girls and 823 boys, aged 11-14 years ($M = 12.2$, $SD = 1.1$), drawn from public junior high schools located in some towns in north eastern Italy. All students were involved in PE as an obligatory course twice a week. Agreement to conduct the study was sought from the headmaster and PE teachers.

Measures

The Task and Ego Orientation in Physical Education Questionnaire

Individual differences in goal orientation were assessed through the Italian version (Bortoli & Robazza, 2005) of the Task and Ego Orientation in Physical Education Questionnaire developed by Walling and Duda (1995). The questionnaire is composed of 16 items included into two scales: eight items are intended to assess an individual's disposition for the ego orientation, and eight items are meant to gauge an individual's disposition for the task orientation. Students responded on a five-point scale ranging from 1, *strongly disagree*, to 5, *strongly agree*. In this study the reliability α for the ego orientation scale was .90, and for the task orientation scale was .79.

Teacher-Initiated Motivational Climate in Physical Education Questionnaire

An individual's perception of the motivational climate was measured through the Italian version (Bortoli, Robazza, Colella, Morano, Berchicci, & Bertollo, 2006) of the Teacher-Initiated Motivational Climate in Physical Education Questionnaire (Papaioannou, 1998b). The questionnaire is a short version of the Learning and Performance Orientations in Physical Education Classes Questionnaire (Papaioannou, 1994) and it consists of 12 items into two scales referring to perceptions of teacher-initiated motivational climate: six items are related to perceptions of the teacher's emphasis on students' task-involvement, and six items are associated with perceptions of the teacher's emphasis on students' ego-involvement. Students responded on a five-point scale ranging from 1, *strongly disagree*, to 5, *strongly agree*. In this study the reliability α for the performance climate scale was .68 and for the mastery climate scale was .80.

Psychobiosocial States

An IZOF-based assessment of idiosyncratic emotions related to performance is usually accomplished through a stimulus list of pleasant and unpleasant emotional descriptors mainly derived from affect scales described by Watson and Tellegen (1985; see Hanin, 2000). The list is used to help participants choose or generate personal descriptors best describing feelings associated with the competitive experience. Emotion profiling research showed that individuals' emotional adjectives often unveil components related to cognition (e.g., alert and focused), motivation (e.g., determined and motivated), body reactions (e.g., relaxed and tense), and movement reactions (e.g., smooth movements and sharp movements) (Bortoli & Robazza, 2002; Hanin & Stambulova, 2002; Robazza & Bortoli, 2003; Ruiz & Hanin, 2004). Therefore, a holistic assessment of the emotional experience should incorporate each component of a PSB state (i.e., emotional, cognitive, motivational, bodily, kinesthetic, performance, and communicative components of pleasant and unpleasant states).

Based on existing lists of descriptors used to assess emotions in sport (e.g. Hanin, 2000; Robazza & Bortoli, 2003; Robazza, Bortoli, & Hanin, 2004) and PE (Robazza & Bortoli, 2005; Robazza, Bortoli, Carraro, & Bertollo, 2006), the two authors independently identified a number of pleasant and unpleasant adjectives pertaining to each of the seven PSB components. After extensive discussion, adjectives clearly conveying a similar emotional experience were aggregated to form a pleasant or unpleasant item. As a result of this procedure, we identified 28-items, two pleasant and two unpleasant representative of each PSB state. An item was composed by two or three descriptors (e.g., serene, calm, and tranquil) rather than just one descriptor. This format of an item was intended to transmit a clear emotional experience related to PE across participants, notwithstanding the group-based (nomothetic) arrangement of items in a questionnaire.

Examples of pleasant and unpleasant items for each PSB component were: Happy, joyful, cheerful, and Anxious, nervous, worried (emotion); Attentive, alert, focused, and Unfocused, distracted, inattentive (cognition); Motivated, determined, stimulated, and Unmotivated, disengaged (motivation); Energetic, reactive, and Lazy, sluggish, lethargic (bodily reaction); Active, dynamic, and Awkward, clumsy (movement); Capable, proficient, effective, and Doubtful, unsure, uncertain (performance); Socializing, collaborative, and Lonely, isolated (communication). For each item, students rated a five-point scale ranging from 0, *not at all*, to 4, *very, very much*.

Procedure

Cooperation from the PE teachers and students was obtained after having explained them the general purposes of the study. Assessment was conducted in small groups of four or five participants involved in PE lessons, and took place in a secluded location near to the PE facilities. Participants who volunteer for the study were ensured about confidentiality. They were presented with the anti-social desirability instructions emphasizing the need for honesty and then asked to complete the questionnaires.

Data Analysis

Descriptive statistics were computed for all measures and data were preliminarily examined to check the assumptions of normality, linearity, multicollinearity, and homogeneity of variance-covariance matrices through frequency and scatter plots, and Box's M-test. To examine the factorial structure of PSB states, the 28-item scale was subjected to exploratory and confirmatory factor analyses. To this purpose, the whole sample ($N = 1632$) was split randomly into two equal groups of 816 participants homogeneous in number by gender and age, so to have a calibration sample and a validation sample. Correlation analysis, hierarchical multiple regression, and canonical correlation were then performed to examine the univariate and multivariate relationships among motivational climate, dispositional orientation, and PSB states. Finally, multivariate analysis of variance (MANOVA) was executed to examine possible gender differences on dispositional goal orientations, motivational climate, and PSB states.

RESULTS

Descriptive Statistics

Means and standard deviations of goal orientations, motivational climate, and pleasant/unpleasant PSB states are presented in Table 1. Both girls and boys perceived a high mastery motivational climate associated with their PE classes, were generally highly task-oriented and moderately ego-oriented. Furthermore, they reported higher scores of pleasant states than unpleasant states linked to their PE experience.

Table 1. Descriptive Statistics for Girls (N= 809) and Boys (N = 823)

Variables	Girls		Boys	
	M	SD	M	SD
Task orientation	33.34	4.13	32.71	4.49
Ego orientation	22.43	7.08	23.88	7.51
Mastery climate	23.76	4.15	23.88	4.18
Performance climate	14.81	4.50	15.32	4.51
Pleasant PSB states	17.20	5.27	19.46	5.01
Unpleasant PSB states	3.91	3.61	4.65	4.14

Factor Analysis of Psychobiosocial States

A principal components factor analysis with oblimin rotation was performed on the data of the calibration sample. Kaiser-Meyer-Olkin value was .92 indicating sampling adequacy. Results indicated five factors and the total variance accounted for was 54.1%. Items not loading at least 0.40 on a factor, and items loading 0.30 on two or more factors, were eliminated, as were factors defined by less than three items. A further criterion was to retain two items, one pleasant and one unpleasant, representative of each PSB dimension. Based on these criteria, the oblimin rotation produced a two-factor solution accounting for 46.6% of the variance. Seven positive items loaded on the first factor and seven negative items loaded on the second factor.

A confirmatory factor analysis was conducted on the data of the validation sample to evaluate the goodness of fit of the expected two-factor solution. Normalized estimate of Mardia's coefficient was 83.98 for the 14 scale items. This value is below the cut-off point of 224 derived by the formula p(p+2) for estimating the limit of departure from multivariate normality, where p equals the number of observed variables (Bollen, 1989). Furthermore, inspection of the skewness and kurtosis values of the individual items indicated item responses normally distributed. Therefore, the maximum likelihood method of estimation was chosen for the data analysis, as it is appropriate when the data are normally distributed. Findings showed the two-factor solution of the questionnaire to be acceptable. Indeed, the χ^2/df ratio was 3.58 (less than 5.0, Kelloway, 1998), GFI = .95, AGFI = .94, NNFI = .93, CFI = .94 (all fit indices were not less than .90, Hu & Bentler, 1999), and RMSEA = .06 (below .10, Steiger, 1990). The reliability α for the pleasant scale was .84 and for the unpleasant scale was .72.

Correlational Analysis

As shown in Table 2, task orientation and mastery climate correlated positively between themselves and with pleasant PSB states, and negatively with unpleasant states. Ego orientation correlated positively with performance climate and pleasant states, and negatively with unpleasant states. Performance climate showed negative correlations with pleasant states and positive correlations with unpleasant states. Finally, correlation between pleasant states and unpleasant states was negative.

Table 2. Bivariate Correlations Between Variables

Variables	Task orientation	Ego orientation	Mastery climate	Performance climate	Pleasant states
Task orientation	–				
Ego orientation	.19*	–			
Mastery climate	.39*	-.03	–		
Performance climate	-.14*	.18*	-.32*	–	
Pleasant PSB states	.40*	.18*	.30*	-.10*	–
Unpleasant PSB states	-.29*	-.10*	-.17*	.21*	-.36*

* Significant correlation at $p < .01$.

Hierarchical Multiple Regression Analysis

To examine whether dispositional goal orientation and motivational climate would predict PSB states, hierarchical multiple regression was performed. Pleasant state total scores were entered as dependent variable in a first analysis. According to the study's purpose and predictions, the order of entry of the independent variables in the regression model was as follows: task orientation, mastery climate, ego orientation, performance climate were entered in the first, second, third, and fourth steps of the model respectively. In a second analysis, unpleasant state total scores were entered as dependent variable, while the order of entry of the independent variables in the regression model was: ego orientation, performance climate, task orientation, and mastery climate in the first, second, third, and fourth steps of the model respectively.

Regression analysis results are presented in Table 3. Task orientation was a significant predictor of pleasant PSB states accounting for 15.8% of variance. Inclusion of mastery climate and ego orientation significantly added to the explanation of the criterion variance, accounting for a small proportion of more variance (3.9%). Performance climate did not contribute significantly to the regression model. Task orientation was also a significant predictor of unpleasant states accounting for 5.9% of more variance after inclusion of ego orientation and performance climate. The effects of both task and ego orientation were negative. The composite effects of the three variables accounted for 12.1% of variance, whereas mastery climate did not contribute significantly to the model.

Table 3. Summary of Hierarchical Regression Analysis of Dispositional Goal Orientations (Task and Ego) and Motivational Climate (Mastery and Performance) as Predictor of Pleasant and Unpleasant PBS States (N = 1632)

Criterion variables	Steps	Predictor variables in order of entry	R^2	R^2 change	F change (p value)	β	SP^2
Pleasant PBS states	1	Task orientation	.16	.16	.00	.30	.27
	2	Mastery climate	.18	.02	.00	.17	.15
	3	Ego orientation	.20	.02	.00	.13	.13
	4	Performance climate	.20	.00	.22	-.03	-.03
Unpleasant PBS states	1	Ego orientation	.01	.01	.00	-.09	-.08
	2	Performance climate	.06	.05	.00	.18	.17
	3	Task orientation	.12	.06	.00	-.24	-.22
	4	Mastery climate	.12	.00	.49	-.02	-.02

β = standardized beta coefficient (incremental), SP^2 = squared semi-partial correlation coefficient.

Canonical Correlation Analysis

Canonical correlation analysis was used to evaluate the multivariate patterns of relationships between two sets of variables. The first set included dispositional orientation and motivational climate variables (i.e., task orientation, goal orientation, mastery climate, and performance climate), while the second set comprised pleasant or unpleasant PSB variables (i.e., emotion, cognition, motivation, bodily reaction, movement, performance, and communication). Therefore, two canonical analyses were performed to evaluate the relationship between the dispositional/situational variables and either pleasant or unpleasant states. The first analysis yielded three significant canonical functions, whereas the second one revealed two significant functions. For both analyses, however, only the first canonical function was interpreted because correlations between pairs of canonical variates were higher than .30 (Tabachnick & Fidell, 2001). Canonical variate correlations on the second canonical function were lower than .30 (i.e., $Rc = .20$ between dispositional/situational set and pleasant PSB states set, and $Rc = .17$ between dispositional/situational set and unpleasant PSB states set). Canonical analysis results are presented in Table 4. A canonical loading value of .30 and above is usually considered an indication of significant loading (Pedhazur, 1982).

Table 4. Canonical Loadings, Proportion of Variance, Redundancies, and Canonical Correlations between Dispositional Goal Orientation and Motivational Climate Set of Variables and Pleasant and Unpleasant PSB States Set of Variables (N = 1632)

Variable	Pleasant PSB states	Unpleasant PSB states
Dispositional goal orientation and motivational climate set		
Task orientation	-.87	-.83
Ego orientation	-.30	-.25
Mastery climate	-.75	-.54
Performance climate	.28	.61
Proportion of variance	.37	.36
Redundancy	.08	.05
PSB states set		
Emotion	-.83	.59
Cognition	-.63	.75
Motivation	-.77	.78
Bodily reaction	-.60	.18
Movement	-.62	.64
Performance	-.61	.65
Communication	-.62	.56
Proportion of variance	.46	.39
Redundancy	.10	.06
Canonical correlation	.47	.38

Regarding pleasant PSB states, the first canonical function reflected high negative loadings on dispositional task orientation and mastery-involving climate (first set), and moderate to high negative loadings on all PBS states (second set), Wilks' $\lambda = .73$, $\chi^2(28) = 508.86$, $p < .001$. Negative loadings across first and second set of variables indicate a direct relationship. Regarding unpleasant states, the first canonical function yielded negative loadings on dispositional task orientation and mastery-involving climate together with a positive loading on performance-involving climate (first set), and moderate to high positive loadings on most of the PBS states (second set), Wilks' $\lambda = .83$, $\chi^2(28) = 313.20$, $p < .001$.

For both pleasant and unpleasant PBS states, the observed relationships ($Rc = .47$ and .38) between the two canonical variates (first set and second set) indicate that those students who are task-oriented and perceive a mastery-involving climate tend to experience high levels of pleasant states and low levels of unpleasant states. Canonical loadings also suggest that low task orientation combined with a performance-involving climate and low mastery-involving climate is related to unpleasant states. Taken together, findings reflected conceptually coherent links among the students' dispositional task orientation, perception of a mastery-involving climate, and pleasant states, as well as the students' experience of a performance-involving climate and unpleasant states.

Gender Differences

MANOVA was conducted to examine possible gender differences on dispositional goal orientations (task and ego), motivational climate (mastery and performance) and PSB states (pleasant and unpleasant). MANOVA yielded significant results on dispositional goal orientations (Wilks' λ = .98, $F_{2,1629}$ = 15.27, p < .001, partial η^2 = .02, motivational climate (Wilks' λ = 1.00, $F_{2,1629}$ = 3.63, p < .03, partial η^2 = .01), and PSB states (Wilks' λ =.92, $F_{2,1629}$ = 71.11, p < .001, partial η^2 = .08). Univariate follow-up showed that, compared to girls, boys scored higher on ego orientation (M = 23.88 vs. 22.43, $F_{1,1630}$ = 8.72, p < .003, ES = 0.20), performance climate (M = 15.32 vs. 14.81, $F_{1,1630}$ = 5.22, p < .03, ES = 0.11), and pleasant states (M = 19.46 vs. 17.20, $F_{1,1630}$ = 79.54, p < .001, ES = 0.44). On the other hand, boys scored lower than girls on task orientation (M = 32.71 vs. 33.34, $F_{1,1630}$ = 16.08, p < .001, ES = 0.15), and unpleasant states (M = 3.91 vs. 4.65, $F_{1,1630}$ = 14.75, p < .001, ES = 0.19).

DISCUSSION

The aim of this study was to examine the link among achievement goals, perceived motivational climate, and pleasant/unpleasant PBS states. Findings provided support to the expected relationship. Regression analysis revealed task orientation to be the most significant predictor of both pleasant and unpleasant PBS states. From an applied perspective, the positive correlation with pleasant states and the negative correlation with unpleasant states underline the importance to foster a task-involvement motivational climate in the PE context. The contribution of ego orientation was much lower, though correlation coefficients with pleasant and unpleasant states were also positive and negative respectively. The expected link between ego orientation and unpleasant PBS states was not revealed. It should be noted, however, that although the current goal perspective literature draws attention to the positive consequences of an individual's task orientation, research findings do not indicate consistent detrimental effects of ego orientation (see Biddle, 2001; Thomas & Barron, 2006). Indeed, ego-oriented pupils who are also task-oriented or perceive themselves as skillful can be strongly motivated to engage in adaptive behaviors.

To a lesser extent than task orientation, mastery climate was a significant predictor of pleasant PBS states, whereas performance climate was a predictor of unpleasant states. These results seem to be in contrast with Cury et al.' (1996) findings showing intrinsic interest in PE to be influenced by mastery climate more than dispositional task orientation. The authors suggested that situational factors may play a more important role than an individual's goal orientation in compulsory activity such as school PE. More research is necessary to assess the differential and combined effects of motivational climate and goal orientation toward enjoyment, intrinsic interest, and pleasant/unpleasant states related to physical activity.

Canonical correlation analysis revealed a multivariate relationship between motivational factors (task/ego orientation and mastery/performance climate) and PBS states. Specifically, results indicated that high task-oriented pupils who perceived a mastery-involving climate tended to experience high levels of pleasant PBS states and low levels of unpleasant states. Conversely, low task-oriented pupils who perceived a high performance- and low mastery-involving climate tended to experience unpleasant states. The contribution of ego orientation was smaller than task orientation to the multivariate relationship. These results are in line with previous research in the PE setting showing positive effects of task orientation combined with perception of a mastery climate on factors such as self-reported discipline (Papaioannou, 1998a), metacognitive processes (Theodosiou & Papaioannou, 2006), and intrinsic motivation to know, experience stimulation, and attain goals (Standage et al., 2003). Research in the sporting context provided further support for the positive effects of the interaction between task orientation and mastery climate. Ommundsen, Roberts, Lemyre, and Miller (2005) found that young female soccer players who perceived a motivational climate as predominantly mastery-oriented, and who were moderately task-oriented and scored negatively on maladaptive perfectionism, reported a better quality of peer relations. Male players who did not value a task orientation, perceived the climate as predominantly performance-oriented, and showed evidence of maladaptive perfectionism, displayed indices of reduced quality of friendship, as weak companionship with peers and reduced sense of loyalty toward peers.

Ames (1992) argued that students' goal orientation may be influenced by the motivational climate created by what teachers do and say. It seems easier to enhance students' motivation by manipulating the motivational climate rather than trying to change an individual's goal orientation. Some work has supported this idea in PE classes (e.g., Digelidis, Papaioannou, Laparidis, & Christodoulidis, 2003; Wallhead & Ntoumanis, 2004). Teachers have a critical role in planning and applying interventions to promote a mastery-involving motivational climate. They should place emphasis on effort, learning, and improvement, thus enhancing pleasant states. Teachers can also plan individualized learning strategies on the basis of their student's goal disposition and evaluate the effectiveness of an instructional process in aiding individuals to become more task-oriented (Walling & Duda, 1995; Weigand & Burton, 2002).

Study findings revealed gender differences on motivational and PBS variables. Boys were less task-oriented and more ego-oriented than girls, in accordance with previous research conducted in the PE setting (Papaioannou & Kouli, 1999; Bortoli, & Robazza, 2005; Walling & Duda, 1995). The boys' predisposition to be more ego-oriented than girls was in accordance with their tendency to perceive the motivational climate as more performance-oriented (Papaioannou & Kouli, 1999). Boys also reported higher levels of both pleasant and unpleasant psychobiosocial states, suggesting that girls are generally less involved in PE lessons. Yet, overall findings showed that male and female participants reported higher scores in task orientation, mastery climate, and pleasant states compared to the respective scores on ego orientation, performance climate, and unpleasant states. It can be suggested that pupils in general feel that PE lessons are a pleasant experience.

In conclusion, the purpose of the study was to examine the univariate and multivariate links among the individual goal orientation, motivational climate perception, and a range of emotion-related states occurring in the PE context, using the achievement goal theory and the

IZOF model as theoretical frameworks. Such an interactive approach can represent a tool for the study of motivation and emotion in PE and provide a comprehensive understanding of pupils' experience associated with physical activity. Of course, the advantages of adopting different theoretical views need to be further investigated. Moreover, beyond dispositional goal orientation and motivational climate, future research should investigate the effects of additional variables on PBS states and, consequently, on an individual's approach/avoidance tendencies toward PE activities. These include self-efficacy, perceived competence, actual skill levels, and the ability to apply coping strategies to deal with situational demands. Researchers should also examine in more detail the advantages of applying the IZOF model conceptualization on a range of PBS states. To this purpose, there is a need to develop reliable scales, thereby providing an accurate measure of each of the PBS states. As an alternative to questionnaires, idiographic assessment procedures can be employed in order to prompt the individual's identification or generation of those PBS adjectives that are relevant and capable to best describe a personal experience associated with a given activity.

REFERENCES

Ames, C. (1992a). Achievement goals, motivational climate, and motivational processes. In G. C. Roberts (Ed.), *Motivation in sport and exercise* (pp. 161-176). Champaign, IL: Human Kinetics.

Ames, C. (1992b). Classrooms: Goals, structures, and student motivation. *Journal of Educational Psychology, 84,* 261-271.

Biddle, S. J. H. (2001). Enhancing motivation in physical education. In G. C. Roberts (Ed.), *Advances in motivation in sport and exercise* (pp. 101-127). Champaign, IL: Human Kinetics.

Bollen, K. A. (1989). *Structural equations with latent variables.* New York: Wiley.

Bortoli, L., & Robazza, C. (2002). Idiosyncratic performance affect in volleyball referees: an extension of the IZOF-emotion model profiling. *Journal of Sport Behavior, 25,* 115-133.

Bortoli, L., & Robazza, C. (2005). Italian version of the Task and Ego Orientation in Physical Education Questionnaire. *Perceptual and Motor Skills, 101,* 901-910.

Bortoli, L., Robazza, C., Colella, D., Morano, M., Berchicci, M, & Bertollo, M. (2006). *Italian version of the Teacher-Initiated Motivational Climate in Physical Education Questionnaire.* Manuscript submitted for publication.

Chen, A. (2001). A theoretical conceptualization for motivation research in physical education: An integrated perspective. *Quest, 53,* 35-58.

Cury, F., Biddle, S. H., Famose, J. P., Goudas, M., Sarrazin, P., & Durand, M. (1996). Personal and situational factors influencing intrinsic interest of adolescent girls in physical education: A structural equation modelling analysis. *Educational Psychology, 16,* 305-314.

Digelidis, N., Papaioannou, A., Laparidis, K., & Christodoulidis, T. (2003). A one-year intervention in 7th grade physical education classes aiming to change motivational climate and attitudes towards exercise. *Psychology of Sport and Exercise, 4,* 195-210.

Duda, J. L. (1996). Maximizing motivation in sport and physical education among children and adolescents: the case for greater task involvement. *Quest, 48,* 290-302.

Duda, J. L. (2001) Achievement goal research in sport: pushing the boundaries and clarifying some misunderstandings. In G. C. Roberts (Ed.), *Advances in motivation in sport and exercise*. Champaign, IL: Human Kinetics. Pp. 129-182.

Duda, J. L., & Nicholls, J. G. (1992). Dimensions of achievement motivation in schoolwork and sport. *Journal of Educational Psychology, 84*, 290-299.

Hanin, Y. L. (1978). A study of anxiety in sports. In W. F. Straub (Ed.), *Sport psychology: An analysis of athlete behavior* (pp. 236-249). Ithaca, NY: Mouvement.

Hanin, Y. L. (1986). State-trait anxiety research on sports in the USSR. In C. D. Spielberger and R. Diaz-Guerrero (Eds.), *Cross cultural anxiety* (Vol. 3, pp. 45-64). Washington, DC: Hemisphere.

Hanin, Y.L. (1997). Emotions and athletic performance: Individual Zones of Optimal Functioning model. *European Yearbook of Sport Psychology, 1*, 29-72.

Hanin, Y. L. (Ed.). (2000). *Emotions in sport*. Champaign, IL: Human Kinetics.

Hanin, Y. L. (2004). Emotion in sports. In C. D. Spielberger (Ed.). *Encyclopedia of Applied Psychology* (Vol. 1, pp. 739-750). Oxford, UK: Elsevier Academic Press.

Hanin Y. L. (In press). Emotions in sport: Current issues and perspectives. In G. Tenenbaum & R. Eklund (Eds.), *Handbook of Sport Psychology* (3rd ed.). New York: Wiley & Sons.

Hanin, Y. L., & Stambulova, N. B. (2002). Metaphoric description of performance states: An application of the IZOF model. *The Sport Psychologist, 16*, 396-415.

Hu, L., & Bentler, P. M. (1999). Cutoff criteria for fit indexes in covariance structure analysis: conventional criteria versus new alternatives. *Structural Equation Modeling, 6*, 1-55.

Kelloway, E. K. (1998). *Using LISREL for structural equation modeling: A researcher's guide*. Thousand Oaks, CA: Sage.

Nicholls, J. G. (1992). The general and the specific in the development and expression of achievement motivation. In G. C. Roberts (Ed.), *Motivation in sport and exercise* (pp. 31-56). Champaign, IL: Human Kinetics.

Ntoumanis, N., & Biddle, S. J. H. (1999). A review of motivational climate in physical activity. *Journal of Sports Sciences, 17*, 643-665.

Ommundsen, Y., Roberts, G., Lemyre, P.-N., & Miller, B. (2005). Peer relationships in adolescent competitive soccer: Associations to perceived motivational climate, achievement goals and perfectionism. *Journal of Sports Sciences, 23*, 977-989.

Papaioannou, A. (1994). Development of a questionnaire to measure achievement orientations in physical education. *Research Quarterly for Exercise and Sport, 65*, 11-20.

Papaioannou, A. (1998a). Goal perspectives, reasons for being disciplined, and self-reported discipline in physical education lessons. *Journal of Teaching in Physical Education, 17*, 421-441.

Papaioannou, A. (1998b). Students' perceptions of the physical education class environment for boys and girls and the perceived motivational climate. *Research Quarterly for Exercise and Sport, 69*, 267-275.

Papaioannou, A., & Kouli, O. (1999). The effect of task structure, perceived motivational climate and goal orientations on students' task involvement and anxiety. *Journal of Applied Sport Psychology, 11*, 51-71.

Pedhazur, E. J. (1982). *Multiple regression in behavioral research: Explanation and prediction* (2nd ed.). New York: Holt, Rinehart & Winston.

Robazza, C. (2006). Emotion in sport: An IZOF perspective. In S. Hanton & S. D. Mellalieu (Eds.), *Literature reviews in sport psychology* (pp. 127-158). New York: Nova Science.

Robazza, C., & Bortoli, L. (2003). Intensity, idiosyncratic content and functional impact of performance-related emotions in athletes. *Journal of Sports Sciences, 21*, 171-189.

Robazza, C., & Bortoli, L. (2005). Changing students' attitudes towards risky motor tasks: An application of the IZOF model. *Journal of Sports Sciences, 23*, 1075-1088.

Robazza, C., Bortoli, L., Carraro, A., & Bertollo, M. (2006). "I wouldn't do it; it looks dangerous": Changing students' attitudes and emotions in physical education. *Personality and Individual Differences, 41*, 767-777.

Robazza, C., Bortoli, L., & Hanin (2004). Precompetition emotions, bodily symptoms, and task-specific qualities as predictors of performance in high-level karate athletes. *Journal of Applied Sport Psychology, 16*, 151-165.

Roberts, G. C. (2001). Understanding the dynamics of motivation in physical activity: the influence of achievement goals on motivational processes. In G. C. Roberts (Ed.), *Advances in motivation in sport and exercise* (pp. 1-50). Champaign, IL: Human Kinetics.

Ruiz, M. C., & Hanin, Y. L. (2004). Metaphoric description and individualized emotion profiling of performance related states in high-level karate athletes. *Journal of Applied Sport Psychology, 16*, 258–273.

Spray, C. M., Biddle, S. J. H., & Fox, K. R. (1999). Achievement goals, beliefs about the causes of success and reported emotion in post-16 physical education. *Journal of Sports Sciences, 17*, 213-219.

Standage, M., Duda, J. L., & Ntoumanis, N. (2003). Predicting motivational regulations in physical education: The interplay between dispositional goal orientations, motivational climate and perceived competence. *Journal of Sports Sciences, 21*, 631-647.

Steiger, J. H. (1990). Structural model evaluation and modification: An interval estimation approach. *Multivariate Behavioral Research, 25*, 173–180.

Tabachnick, B. G., & Fidell, L. S. (2001). *Using multivariate statistics* (4th ed.). Needham Heights, MA: Allyn & Bacon.

Theodosiou, A., & Papaioannou, A. (2006). Motivational climate, achievement goals and metacognitive activity in physical education and exercise involvement in out-of-school settings. *Psychology of Sport and Exercise, 7*, 361-379.

Thomas, J. A., & Barron, K. E. (2006). A test of multiple achievement goal benefits in physical education activities. *Journal of Applied Sport Psychology, 18*, 114-135.

Treasure, D. C. (2001). Enhancing young people's motivation in youth sport: an achievement goal approach. In G. C. Roberts (Ed.), *Advances in motivation in sport and exercise* (pp. 79-100). Champaign, IL: Human Kinetics.

Wallhead, T. L., & Ntoumanis, N. (2004). Effects of a sport education intervention on students' motivational responses in physical education. *Journal of Teaching in Physical Education, 23*, 4-18.

Walling, M. D., & Duda, J. L. (1995). Goals and their associations with beliefs about success in and perceptions of the purposes of physical education. *Journal of Teaching in Physical Education, 14*, 140-156.

Watson, D., & Tellegen, A. (1985). Toward a consensual structure of mood. *Psychological Bulletin, 98*, 219-235.

Weigand, D. A., & Burton, S. (2002). Manipulating achievement motivation in physical education by manipulating the motivational climate. *European Journal of Sport Science*, 2 (1), 1-14.

INDEX